Second CHANCES

DENNIS ROBINSON

Second CHANCES

One man's fight to regain
his Faith, Family, and Future

DENNIS ROBINSON

Editors: Donna Melillo, Adam Tillinghast, Kayte Middleton
Cover Design: Jason Kauffmann / Firelight Interactive / firelightinteractive.com
Interior Design: Rick Soldin / book-comp.com

Indigo River Publishing
3 West Garden Street Ste. 352
Pensacola, FL 32502
www.indigoriverpublishing.com

Ordering Information:
Quantity sales: Special discounts are available on quantity purchases by corporations, associations, and others. For details, contact the publisher at the address above.
Orders by U.S. trade bookstores and wholesalers: Please contact the publisher at the address above.

Printed in the United States of America

Publisher's Cataloging-in-Publication Data is available upon request.
Library of Congress Control Number: 2013942082

Print ISBN 978-0-9891263-7-3
Digital ISBN 978-0-9891263-9-7

First Edition

With Indigo River Publishing, you can always expect great books, strong voices, and meaningful messages.
Most importantly, you'll always find ... words worth reading.

First and foremost, I want to dedicate this book to my Lord and Savior, Jesus Christ, who paid the ultimate price for my sin.

I would also like to dedicate it to the love of my life, the mother of my children, and my wonderful wife, Peggy. I have never seen a more selfless person who puts the needs of others before her own. Thank you for being there for me through all the trials I have put you through. I love you more than words can say.

I also dedicate this book to my children and their spouses. Thank you for all you have done for us; we love you very much. And lastly, we dedicate this book to both Peggy's and my parents who have encouraged and stood behind us.

Contents

Foreword

I am privileged to call Dennis and Peggy Robinson my friends. We are also co-laborers as we serve together as missionaries with Continental Baptist Missions. The Robinsons truly exemplify a servant's spirit. Their love and faithfulness to the Lord Jesus Christ is demonstrated through their service to the local church as they construct buildings for His glory. It's exciting to watch God use them!

The first time I heard Dennis speak, we were serving as guest speakers in a missions conference in Minnesota. The former dairy farmer informed the congregation that he wasn't a preacher—in fact, he may have said, "I ain't no preacher." Yet when he opened the scriptures, I was riveted. It was not so much his oratory skills, sermon structure, or polished

presentation that engaged me. Rather, I was gripped, edified, and blessed by his simple and accurate handling of the
Word of God. As he told his story of divinely-gifted *Second
Chances,* I felt as though the Lord held my heart in His
hands and was gently massaging it with spiritual truth.

I was blessed as I read *Second Chances.* Here is the
modest, yet powerful story of an ordinary man willing to be
used of God in an extraordinary way. Yet more so, it is the
story of a loving God who would take extreme measures to
draw his child closer to Himself and into His service. The
Lord spared Dennis' life, but that's not the end of the story.

Second Chances will encourage you to carefully eval-
uate your walk with a loving and compassionate Savior.
As Dennis tells his story with the goal of giving God the
glory, I believe you will be edified and challenged as you are
reminded of God's personal role in your life. He cares—*He
really does!* It is my prayer that you'll be encouraged to
examine your personal relationship with Jesus Christ and
walk accordingly.

Bill Jenkin III
President—Continental Baptist Missions

Preface

Most people, when they have a brush with death, say that they saw their life flash before their eyes. I didn't see my childhood; I didn't see Peggy and me as newlyweds; and I didn't see any of my children growing up. I didn't see any of that. I just remember begging for my life—I cried out loud, "God, I don't want to die!"

"You Pant! I'm Having this Baby!"

I grew up the second of five D's in the Robinson clan—Don, Dennis, Debby, David, and Darrel. If you think that's hard to say, our middle names are just as bad … Donald James, Dennis John, Debby Jean, David Joel, and Darrel Jon! We were an interesting bunch. I can't remember much from my early childhood, but my earliest memories were about living on a farm with Dad and the rest of the family.

My dad was raised on a diary farm and planned to be a farmer the rest of his life. However, the promise of a high-paying job and a warmer climate prompted him to sell their cows and farm equipment and move to Florida. The high pay didn't materialize; and coupled with homesickness, we moved back to Wisconsin after two years.

Dad worked in a pallet factory and became very active in a small country church. As he heard God's Word preached, and through intense Bible study, Dad felt God calling him to the ministry. In 1962, when I was five, my parents headed south again—with four small children and the fifth on the way. This time, it was to Lakeland, Florida, where Dad enrolled in Florida Baptist Institute and Seminary, where he spent the next five years preparing for the ministry.

While Dad was in school, the Lord started working on my mom, and she realized that she did not have a personal relationship with Jesus Christ. During a revival service, she accepted the Lord as her personal Savior.

In 1966, we moved back to Wisconsin where Dad became the pastor of his first church. My brothers and I were so excited to move back to Wisconsin! One of the biggest things we looked forward to was going deer hunting with Dad and Grandpa.

One year, Dad thought it would be great if we had a camper to stay in during hunting season; it would make life easier for Grandma since we could stay in the camper instead of her house. He bought an old Volkswagen minivan and converted it into a camper for us. The day finally came when we got to use it for the first time. I couldn't wait! We got to the park and set up camp. I don't remember exactly how cold it was, but I remember that we had to run a heater to stay warm. There were just two problems with this camper situation. First, when we turned the heater on, the condensation built up inside the camper and started to rain down on us—not fun when you're trying to sleep! The other big problem was that every hour someone had to go outside to use the restroom. With that many people crowded in a small space, everyone woke up when someone had to go. Needless to say, it was a short night, nobody got any sleep, and we *never* used that "camper" again!

Like every kid growing up, I lived for summer. The highlight was going to Uncle Wayne and Aunt Donna's farm for a week or two. There I would get to drive the tractor or help feed the cows. I absolutely loved being on the farm—among all the animals and machinery. There was so much to do and see (and smell) ... There was always something new to do. After all, what kid doesn't like to drive a tractor?

Not only did Uncle Wayne farm, but he also had a milk route. He would pick up milk from all the local farmers and take it to the creamery where they would make it into cheese. I used to love riding the route with him!

One summer while I was on the farm, Mom and Dad asked my uncle to give me a haircut. Back then, we wore our hair very short. I hated it at the time, but now I prefer it that way—low maintenance! Well, Uncle Wayne thought he would be funny, so he gave me a mohawk. Then we jumped in the truck and ran the milk route. We got some good laughs along the way, but the best one was when we stopped to see my grandma. I thought she was going to die laughing when she saw me! Needless to say, we went home and shaved the rest of it off before my mom and dad saw me!

In November of 1976, my family moved to the small community of Hillsdale, Wisconsin, where my dad became the new pastor of First Baptist Church. It was a farming area, and most of the folks in the church were involved with some sort of agriculture. It was a perfect match: Dad had a farming background, and I had wanted to farm since I was just a little kid. I was in my late teens and I knew I would like it there, but I soon fell in love with more than the farming community.

The first time I saw Peggy was at church. We became friends right away; and except for one short breakup because of me and my stupidity, we were virtually inseparable. While we were dating, Peggy's dad invited my family over for dinner after church one Sunday. Peggy and her three sisters had worked so hard to make the meal; but alas, it was just not meant to be. Among other problems, the roast ended up like shoe leather—extremely tough. I think the best part was when her dad took a drink of the "juice" and went running out the front door. Come to find out, it was straight tonic water! As Peggy and I like to say about these kinds of situations, "We made memories."

After dating for about a year, Peggy and I were fairly serious in our relationship—serious enough that we were planning to elope. However, small-town "news" had a way of getting around quite effectively. Once our plans to elope got out, we changed our plans. On December 8, 1977, we had a small family wedding and started our lives together. I may not have been a starry-eyed romantic at that point, but I certainly didn't expect the speed bumps to come along so fast! The morning after the wedding, when we woke up at the hotel, the wind chill was negative fifty degrees. Not only that, but it cost us fifty bucks to get our old car started! We thought, "Real life, here we come!"

We had planned to move to Richland Center, Wisconsin, where I grew up, and we had both been promised jobs there. Unfortunately, when the time came to start, both jobs were gone. All I can say is we lived on love for the first couple of months of our lives together.

We both wanted to have our kids right away, so we were thrilled when we found out we were expecting our first little one! During the pregnancy, the only food that Peggy could keep down was watermelon. The problem was that it was the dead of winter—naturally, we had an extremely hard time finding them. When we *were* able to find them, we had to pay a premium price. Regardless, we made it through.

Another fond memory of our early days together was late that first winter. Peggy was sick from morning sickness and the smell of fuel oil from the heater in our little house.

She decided to surprise me by having a great supper waiting for me when I got home from working at the feed mill. Well, just about everything went wrong with the meal! The meat tasted like shoe leather (yum!), the vegetables were not fully cooked, and nothing seemed to be going right. (Sound familiar?) When it came time for dessert, she knew at least *that* would be good! After all, how can you ruin apple pie? When I took a bite, she asked, "Well, what do you think?" I told her that it was "different"—it definitely had a strange taste to it.

Hazel, a dear, old lady friend of ours, had given us some of her canned goods. When Peggy told Hazel that she made an apple pie with the canned apples, Hazel got a puzzled look on her face and said that she had not given Peggy any canned apples. When Peggy described the jar to her, all Hazel could do was laugh. Come to find out those were not canned apples, but pickled watermelon rind. I guess my taste buds weren't broken after all!

On October 3, 1978, our Amy Marie came into our world. She was our little bundle of joy! She was the second granddaughter for my side of the family, and she was the first for Peggy's side. Looking back, I have to say that Peggy gave her the ride of her life the day before she was born. First, we rode a motorcycle to an auction; I guess that is a "no-no" for an expectant mother. Then, when we got home from that, she climbed 70 feet up the outside of the silo to see how full it was.

Finally, she went out to get the cows so we could start milking. The problem was that when she got out to the pasture, all the cows were in the hay field. Peggy went to work rounding all of them up and trying to get them back where they belonged in the pasture. As she was running across the field, she tripped and fell face first, landing directly on her stomach. Needless to say, Amy was born the next day ...

We started our farming experience less than a year after our wedding by going to work for Bob, Peggy's dad. We were there about a year. They say it's hard to work for family members—we definitely had our ups and downs, but we also gained a lot of knowledge about farming.

Around this same time, I realized that I had been a
fake in my spiritual life. Even though I grew up in a pastor's
home, I did not have a *personal* relationship with God. I
was missing heaven by eighteen inches—I had a *"head"*
knowledge of God, but I did not have Him in my *heart*.
After hearing a message on the Christian radio station we
often listened to while doing chores in the barn and then
attending a concert and hearing the message in both song
and word, I went to talk with my folks. I got down on my
knees and prayed and asked Christ to come into my life
and forgive me of my sins.

We spent the next few years working as hired help
on several farms throughout northern Wisconsin, and they
all had their highs and lows. As hired help, we often were
given jobs that no one else wanted to do. That being said,
we still enjoyed each farm we had the opportunity to work
on, and we definitely learned from all of them.

On December 31, 1979, our first son, Richard Francis,
was born. He was named after my dad and Peggy's dad and
grandpa. He came into this world just 1½ hours short of
being a New Year's baby. I told Peggy to pant and hold on,

but she told me, "*You* pant! I'm having this baby!" Obviously, she won. Rich was the first grandson for both sides of our families.I wanted Rich to be born on New Year's Day for two reasons. First, the first baby born for the year gets some nice presents. Second, my dad's birthday is January 1st.

The first major trauma in our lives came April 23, 1980 when Peggy's sister, Penny, was killed in a tragic farming accident. I was driving a tractor, getting a field ready to plant when my mom, dad, and Peggy pulled in and said we needed to talk. During the brief seconds I was driving to them, I knew something was wrong. I just didn't think it could be nearly as bad as it turned out to be.

Penny was only fifteen years old. We asked why God would allow such a thing to happen! Though it was hard to lose a family member, we knew that someday we would see Penny again because there was a point in her life that she had accepted Christ and became a child of God.

The next major event of our marriage was when Amy's kidneys suddenly shut down for fourteen days. She was only eighteen months old at the time. The doctors did dialysis by hand and were on the verge of sending her to a children's hospital in Minnesota when all of a sudden Amy's kidneys started working again. Peggy stayed by her side the whole time she was in the hospital. The only time she went home was on a Sunday, the day before the doctors planned to send her to the children's hospital, so she could shower and freshen up. When we got back to the hospital, the receptionist told us that Amy Robinson had passed 4 ounces of urine. The funny part was the receptionist had no idea we were Amy's parents. I think she was just so excited to share that Amy was doing better. Miraculously, Amy's kidneys started working on their own. We believe her recovery was the Lord's answer to all of the prayers that were offered on her behalf. In fact, her kidneys came back one hundred percent, and she hasn't had any problems since.

These speed bumps seemed huge to us at the time. Little did we know we were just getting started!

Do I Have Your Attention Yet?

$\mathcal{L}$ooking back now, I see that the first time God really tried to get my attention was in January of 1981. At the time, Peggy and I were working for another farmer. One particular Sunday, I got up early to help the farmer with the morning chores. After attending the morning service, I left Peggy and our two kids at my parents' house while I went back to the farm to do the afternoon chores. Once they were done, I headed back to church for the evening service. I remember that the passenger door of the mid-1960's International truck I had restored was not shut tight. I also remember it being extremely cold, typical for January in Wisconsin. It had been a long day; I was tired; but the truck was still nice and warm.

Back at my parents' house, Peggy noticed it was getting late, and realized I should have gotten there already. Suddenly, a knock came at the back door of my folks' home. It was a stranger asking if she could use the phone to call for an ambulance because of a bad wreck. After making the call, the stranger asked if my parents had some old blankets to cover the guy in the truck because he was badly hurt. She didn't know if he was going to make it. Peggy looked at my dad and said, "That's Dennis." Dad asked, "How do you know?" Peggy told him that she just knew in her heart that it was me.

She was right. While I was driving, I fell asleep behind the wheel. I suddenly woke up as my truck was veering toward the ditch. I jerked the wheel back, but I over-corrected, slamming into a car head-on. I was thrown out through the passenger door that was not shut all the way.

Peggy, Mom, Dad, and my brother Dave rushed to the accident site. When Dave got there, he started freaking out. I had to calm *him* down—go figure! Apparently, I looked worse off than I actually was. My knee was in excruciating pain, but I knew I wasn't going to die. Soon, the ambulance arrived and took me to the hospital. As I waited to be examined by the doctors, I kept telling Peggy that I needed a drink. Peggy kept telling me to be quiet because she didn't want them to think I was an alcoholic. Of course, I meant a drink of water, but the police officers around me wouldn't have known that.

Finally, the doctors came to see me. They examined me and took some x-rays. Then they tried to get me to walk. That proved to be impossible as my knee was in way too much pain. After a few days, the doctors wanted to send me home, but Peggy knew she would not be able to take care of two very small children and me at the same time. Besides that, she was also expecting our third child. The doctors let me stay; and on Thursday, a specialist came to look at my knee.

It was ultimately decided that I would need to be transferred to the hospital in Eau Claire, Wisconsin, to have knee surgery. My knee was so badly torn that the doctor could take my leg and turn it completely sideways—legs shouldn't be able to do that! Because they were not able to repair most of the damage on the inside of my knee, all they could do was staple the damaged nerves and tendons to the bone.

It took me six months to recover. I was a very miserable person throughout this time. I needed to be out working—providing for my family. I know now that God was trying to get my attention. Yet, I pursued my own interests, even as I was recovering. I was still drawn to farming, and as I recovered, I worked at a small engine shop—something I really enjoyed. However, my desires were still not His plan.

While I was recovering, our third and final child came to us on August 8, 1981. We named him after me, Dennis John, but he goes by John. As I said, I was working at a small engine shop. However, what I *didn't* mention was that it was five hours away from where we were living at the time. My sister and brother-in-law (Debby & Kevin) let me stay with them during the week, and I drove home each weekend. This particular weekend, I made it most of the way home, but ran out of gas and had no money on me to get more. I had to call Peggy, who had to get Amy and Rich out of bed and drive 40 miles one way to come help me get home. It was around 2:30 in the morning before we got home; John was born 12 hours later.

This completed our family. It was kind of neat: Amy was born in October, the same month as Peggy. Rich was born the day before my dad's birthday, and John was born the day before my birthday.

We had a fairly normal family, but we went through the bumps, bruises, cuts, and scrapes that any family with three rambunctious young kids would go through.

A few months after the accident, Peggy and I bought a cattle hauling business. This would ultimately prove to be another way I feel God was trying to get my attention. Local farmers would call us to come to their farms and pick up any livestock they wanted to sell. We would take them to either the local sales barn or the larger stockyards in South Saint Paul, Minnesota. We would also move livestock to the pasture, take them to the fair for showing, or do any other transporting of cattle a farmer needed done. We stayed very busy between farm work and the cattle hauling.

On one trip to Saint Paul, I had more livestock to haul than usual. Because of this, I took our big truck, and Peggy followed me with the pickup and trailer. Looking back, I feel God was once again trying to get my attention. As we got closer to the stock yards, I began to feel ill; the closer we got, the worse I became. I was sneezing, having a hard time breathing, and feeling very sick to my stomach. Once we arrived, I was too sick to do anything. Peggy had to take charge of getting everything off the truck.

It was hot outside, but I knew the sales pavilion was air-conditioned. I thought if I could just sit in the air conditioning for a few minutes, I might start feeling better. The sales pavilion, however, was located in the middle of the stock yards. In order to get there, I had to walk on a catwalk above all the pens the cattle were held in. I finally made it to the pavilion, and Peggy met me there. I sat in the building for a while, but I still wasn't feeling any better. On my way to the restroom, I asked Peggy to find out where the closest hospital was. When I came out of the restroom, I just couldn't take another step and collapsed to the ground—someone called 9-1-1, and two paramedic teams quickly arrived. They started working on me, but by then, they had a hard time finding a pulse. They got me stabilized and finally loaded me into an ambulance. The poor driver had no place to turn around, so to get out of the sales barn, he had to back out all of the way through the cattle pens.

Once at the hospital, it was determined that I had a severe allergic reaction to cattle dander. The doctor spoke with Peggy and, during the course of their conversation, suggested that we find a new occupation. Peggy told the doctor that we had just bought the business, and with what we had paid for it, we couldn't afford to quit. The doctor asked Peggy what she thought her husband was worth. Peggy just looked at him and asked what he meant. He said that the next time, I might not be so lucky—I might not make it to the hospital.

We knew we couldn't afford to stop hauling cattle, so we chose the business over my health and continued to haul cattle for another five years. The Lord was definitely watching over us, and I never had another allergic reaction like that. Again, God was trying to get my attention, but I still wouldn't listen. I had my own dreams to pursue.

"They Almost had the Fire Out."

*F*rom an early age, I always wanted to farm—our ultimate goal was to be full-time farmers. Purchasing the cattle hauling business was a step in the right direction, but owning our own farm was our real dream. That's why it was such a very special day when we purchased our first "hobby" dairy farm. It was a forty-acre parcel with a barn and an old farm house. We purchased it from Bob and Sue, Peggy's dad and step-mom; they played a huge part in helping us get started on our own.

Before we could start producing and selling milk from our dairy cows, a state official had to come to our farm and inspect just about everything. Our barn had been used to house young livestock for many years and needed some serious work, to say the least. There was so much to do, but finally it was for us and not someone else. First, we used a bobcat to clean out a center aisle. Then we forked and shoveled out almost 70 *loads* of bedding and manure from the stalls. Not only did we have to remove all the buildup, but then we had to wash and clean everything from top to bottom. We also had to build a milk house in the barn to house the milk tank and the other milking equipment. When all that work was done, we had the inspector come back for an evaluation. It was a great day when he gave us the go-ahead to start milking!

Dairy farms produce two grades of milk. Grade B milk is used for making cheese, and Grade A is used to make cheese or is bottled and sold at the stores. Because the requirements are not as strict for Grade B, we started out on that. However, you get paid more money for Grade A. Farmers get paid for every hundred pounds of milk they produce. The sad part is that most of the time, it just barely pays the bills—if even that.

One day as I was out in the yard, I saw the milkman who hauled our milk to the factory. He was just pulling out from our neighbor's farm, heading over to ours. I wondered why my neighbor got more money for his milk than I got for mine, and yet the milkman put it all together on the same truck. That was it for me—we immediately went to work getting our farm set up so we could be on Grade A too. We had the field man from our creamery come out and look over our barn to let us know what we needed to do. During this inspection, we learned about a new law stating that the inside walls of the barn had to have a flat, smooth surface on them. Our old barn was made up of two-foot-thick stone walls. We had to put wood framing all around the inside of the barn, put plywood on the framing, and paint everything white. Looking back, it's kind of funny; our veterinarian, Al, who took care of our cattle's health needs, kept telling us that we would never be able to get to Grade A. I think he did it just to prod us to get it done. After a lot of work, we had the inspector come back again, and we finally got to Grade A—another milestone in the life of a farmer.

Our goal all along was that I would be able to stop working away from the farm and work full-time, side by side, with Peggy and the kids. We were slowly building up our herd; finally heading in that direction.

A little side story here: As some farmers do, we would look for alternative feed options for our cows in order to save money. One such option was potatoes. We would have a semi-load of scraps brought in from the processing plant, and then we would use a wheelbarrow to haul them into the barn and feed them to the cows.

One particular morning, Peggy was milking, and I was feeding the cows. I had filled the wheelbarrow and headed to the barn. The next thing I knew, Peggy was asking me where I was headed. I guess I zoned out and was halfway down the driveway. It was hard enough to haul those potatoes without going out of my way with them ...

After five years, I closed the cattle hauling business since a lot of farmers in our area were quitting and business was dropping off. In order to have health insurance for my family, I started to work at a cheese factory. I would work twelve-hour shifts, two days on and then two days off. I worked the night shift so we could still get our farming done during the day. As you will find out a little later, having the health insurance ended up being a huge blessing.

Farming in a rural community has its advantages, but it also has its disadvantages. On Christmas Eve in 1985, in the middle of the night, an electrical fire started in our house. The fire truck arrived, but they had to get water out of the river. That winter wasn't forgiving—the wind chill was a negative 50 degrees, and the river was frozen! The fire fighters had to cut a hole in the ice to get to the water. Because it was so cold, they also had a really hard time keeping their equipment running. They almost had the fire out and just needed one more load of water when the truck broke down. The fire continued to grow, and we lost our entire house and all of our belongings. Though we lost all of these earthly possessions and photos, we were thankful to God for sparing our lives that night.

The lack of fire hydrants was definitely a disadvantage of living in a rural farm community; however, the advantage is that news spreads quickly. The next day, Elton Hoff, a dear friend of ours, opened the church doors and sat there the *entire* Christmas Day to receive clothing, food, toys, blankets, and other donations from the community. We were so thankful for everyone's support as we began to rebuild our lives.

That next spring and summer, we found ourselves extremely busy between working at the factory, farming, and building a new home. We hired a builder with the agreement that we would do as much of the labor as we could. Our families were a huge help through this time as well. My brother assisted with the wiring, Peggy's sisters watched the kids as we worked, and we lived in my parents' basement until the house was complete.

Once we settled into our new home, the desire to be farming full-time continued to grow. Peggy and I loved working and being together. We knew our little farm could not support us full-time, but we were not sure how to move to the next step of being self-supported.

Around the same time, my in-laws purchased a farm about two miles from us that was set up just the way we wanted ours to be. Also during this time, Peggy's dad had his hip replaced, making it difficult for him to use the stairs in his old farm house. Since we built our new home all on one level, we worked out a deal with Bob and Sue to trade farms. We would go to the bigger farm with more land but a much older home, and they would move to the smaller farm with the newer, one-level house.

Moving day was quite the day, and once again, our families were a huge part of it. Our family moved both households while Peggy, Bob, and I moved the cows and milking equipment. It was a sight to see! They would load the truck with things from our house and take it over to the new farm. Then they would load the truck with Bob and Sue's things and bring them back to the new house. They did this all day long. At the end of the day, when we finally got done with the milking that night, we walked into our house that had been set up by family. We had to look around to find where they had unpacked everything, but we were very thankful.

As time went on and our kids were growing, a young man named Dan started to show up at our door step. We knew his family a little. He did have a farming background after all, so he couldn't be *all* bad. The day eventually came when he asked our permission to marry our daughter, Amy. What was I to say? Actually, it didn't matter what I said. They were in love, and they were going to get married. I am so glad God gave us only one daughter. Walking down that long, long aisle to give my daughter away was one of the hardest things I have ever done.

They decided to have the song "Butterfly Kisses" played before I gave her to Dan. To this day, I am still unable to hear that song without bawling my eyes out. In fact, one day while I was feeding the cows, Peggy came outside and caught me wiping my eyes. She asked what was wrong, and I told her that "Butterfly Kisses" just finished playing on the radio. She just shook her head and went back to milking the cows.

"June 9, 1998, Looked Like it was Going to be a Good Day."

*T*hroughout this time, I became very bitter toward God over many things that had happened not only in my life, but also in the lives of other family members. I felt guilty for not being home with my family more and I was bitter toward God for a personal situation that involved family that I will not go into. My walk with God had dwindled down to nothing.

As a result, I had allowed work to become my god. I would justify it by saying I needed to provide for my family. I would work all night at the cheese factory, go home to sleep for a couple of hours, and then go out and work all day on the farm. Then, I would take a two or three hour nap and then go back to the factory and start all over again.

I had taken God and put Him in a jar with the lid on tight. I told Him if He left me alone, I would leave Him alone. As I said before, I was a very bitter man. Peggy would ask me what was wrong, and I would tell her that she just wouldn't understand. The bitterness had welled up inside me so much, that it consumed my life. I was at such a low point, that while working under some equipment, I prayed that it would just fall on me and put me out of my misery.

One day, I had been working nonstop on an old piece of farm machinery, trying to get it to work. No matter what I did, it just would not go. I *had* to get this machine fixed, or we wouldn't be able to harvest the hay, and we would lose the whole crop. Finally, I stormed out of the field to find Peggy. I told her if we were going to get the hay harvested, I had to go find something that would actually work. It was much later that I realized the real issue, however, had nothing to do with farm equipment—the bigger problem was internal. The storm inside me was still brewing, and I hadn't done anything yet to get things right with God. Peggy actually told me that day, "I don't know what it's going to take to get a hold of you." As she walked away, she broke down and began to pray. She prayed, "God, what is it going to take to get a hold of him? Lord, he's Yours." You see, Peggy had been trying to change me. She saw the bitterness in my life. She saw the way it was eating at me; she just didn't know how deep it really was. That day, she made a decision to let go. She knew she couldn't change me; only God could. Little did she know that her prayer was about to get answered … but not in the way she expected.

The next day, we ended up driving about 100 miles to purchase a used chopper. I was so excited about being able to get our crops in and not having to spend valuable time fixing the equipment!

June 9, 1998, looked like it was going to be a good day. Because I had worked the night before at the cheese factory, I took a nap for a couple of hours when I got home, then headed out to start chopping hay. I bought the hay from my father-in-law, so we were over on his land about a half-mile up the road from our place. Peggy was in town for the day to work on some apartment buildings where she did general upkeep and yard work. John, our teenage son, and Tony, one of the neighbor boys, were helping me with the field work.

When harvesting hay, the hay first gets cut down; then it sits for a day or two to dry. It gets run through a chopper, which cuts it into fine pieces and throws it into a wagon before it's taken to the barn. Next, the hay is unloaded into a blower. This blower has paddles that help break up the hay to make it easier to send into the silo, where it is stored until being fed to the cows in the winter. That day, I was chopping the hay, and the boys were taking the wagons back down to our farm and unloading the wagons into the silo.

Things were going fairly well until one of the wagons broke down. I should have taken the time to fix it right then. Instead, I just parked it and borrowed another one from a friend of ours. The rest of the day went pretty well. As it got later, the weather started to shift, and it looked like it could rain any time. We needed to get the rest of the hay off the ground, before it rained, or we would have had to wait until it dried out. We worked quickly and loaded nearly all the hay before it started raining. While the boys made their last trip back to our farm, I hurried through the final load of hay, using the wagon I had borrowed. I had not been filling it that full before because it was old, and I knew I needed to take it easy with that wagon.

As I pulled the load down into the driveway of the farm, Peggy pulled in behind me, having just finished with her work in town. We chatted for a couple of minutes, and she said she was going in to grab a sandwich before she went down to start milking the cows. I didn't know it at the time, but John and Tony had gone out to get the cows to start the evening chores; this would work out to be a blessing.

I pulled the wagon into place to start unloading. There is a shaft between the tractor and the wagon called the power takeoff. It powers the equipment in the wagon to pull the load to the front and sends the hay to the blower. As I turned on the power takeoff, I heard a loud BANG! I stopped unloading the wagon and got off the tractor to go see what happened. What I found was that the apron, the chain that pulled the hay to the front of the wagon for unloading had broken. This made me so angry because it was the wagon that I had borrowed. I thought to myself, "I should have known it would break—I *borrowed* it!"

I want to take a minute to explain what a chopper box is. For lack of better words, it is a box on wheels. Only its front is open, and there are three augers across this opening. There are little triangular-shaped pieces of metal welded to the augers that help break up the load—these played a very important part in what happened later. There is an "apron" on the floor of the chopper box. As you

unload the hay out of the wagon, it pulls the load slowly to the front. The augers break the hay up and drop it into a fourth auger that sends it through the blower.

As a workaholic, with bitterness building up inside me and exhaustion setting in from lack of sleep, I wasn't thinking straight. I knew that I needed to get the hay out of the wagon in order to fix what had broken, so I decided to shut off the apron but let the augers keep turning. Then I got a pitchfork and stood on a pipe that went across the front of the wagon as a support.

I can't remember exactly what happened next. In the back of my mind, I vaguely remember that as the augers were turning, I was pulling the hay out from the front and the pitchfork got tangled up in the auger. I'm sure this didn't help my attitude at all. I should have seen it as a warning from God. I found another pitchfork and started again to pull the hay out of the wagon. The more I pulled out, the farther I had to reach in to get it. I was wearing a long-sleeve sweater because the temperature was a little cool. As I reached in, my sweater caught on one of the triangular pieces, and the auger started pulling me over the front of the wagon between the top and middle augers.

There are two things that I can remember at this point—like it was yesterday. The first was thinking about how I would stay out of the blower. I knew that if I got down into that, it would dice me into a thousand pieces. Whatever they did find of me up in the silo would be carried out in a five-gallon pail.

Most people, when they have a brush with death, say they saw their life flash before their eyes. I didn't see my childhood; I didn't see Peggy and myself as newlyweds; and I didn't see any of my children growing up. I didn't see any of that. I just remember begging for my life. I cried out loud, "God, I don't want to die!" Suddenly, I didn't want Him to be sitting on that shelf, in a jar with the lid on tight anymore. I wanted Him to come and get me out of the trouble that I had gotten myself into. I had let so much bitterness and anger build up in me. I know He had every right to let me die that day. Ironically, that's what I *thought* I wanted. I had been at a point in my life before where I *wanted* a machine to fall on me and kill me. Deep inside, though, I didn't want to leave my family. I didn't want to die—I wanted to *live*.

Shortly after crying out to God, the augers suddenly stopped turning. The tractor was still running; the power takeoff was still turning; yet the augers stopped. By this time, I had been pulled between the augers all the way down to my waist. Somehow, I managed to turn the augers backward to free my stomach. Once free of the augers, I turned myself around and sat on the front of the wagon. I knew I couldn't jump down nor could I step down on the power takeoff. I put my arm in the hole in my belly and started yelling for help. I yelled a couple of times before I started thinking that no one could hear me back there. I was out behind the barn, and Peggy was up at the house. I didn't know where John and Tony were. Besides that, there were two tractors running, making all kinds of noise.

I can also remember thinking for some reason that they wouldn't keep me at Barron, our local hospital. I figured I would end up an hour away at the hospital in Eau Claire for a short time; then I would be back to work. Despite those thoughts, I continued to yell for help. Finally, John came running to me. After shutting the tractor off, he helped get me down off of the wagon and sat me on the power takeoff shaft that went from the tractor to the wagon.

Speaking with John years later, he shared with us his side of what happened. As I mentioned earlier, he and Tony had gone out to get the cows from the pasture. He told us that he was upset because the mini-bike wouldn't start, so they had to ride their bicycles out into the pasture. This ended up being a blessing because he would not have heard me calling for help if he had been on the mini-bike. The noise of the motor running would have been too loud.

He also told us that he did not hear a distinct yell. What he heard sounded more like a cat in distress. He said it was as if God told him that something was wrong. John asked Tony if he heard the noise. He said no, but John knew something was wrong. They jumped on the bikes and rode back down toward the barn. In order to get across the stream that ran through the barnyard, they jumped off of the bikes and ran the rest of the way on foot.

After John got me down off of the wagon and sitting, I told him he needed to call 9-1-1 from the barn and then go get Peggy. The first time he dialed, it wouldn't go through (at that time we still had a rotary phone in the barn). He knew he needed to slow down a little, and the second time, it went through. He did a great job explaining what happened and where we were.

An interesting side note to this is that the head of our local county jail, Mark, was in the dispatch room when the call came in. Mark knew John because Lisa, his daughter, and John went to the same Christian school. John and Lisa eventually got married, and Mark is now his father-in-law.

John then went running up to the house to get Peggy. She said that she remembered seeing a shadow flying by the window, and then John was at the door telling her that she needed to come immediately. He told her that I was hurt and that he didn't know if I would still be alive when they got back down to me.

They both came running to help. I told Peggy to get some towels to wrap around me to help stop the bleeding. John ran back to the house and grabbed a hand-full of towels. While getting the towels, John took the time to call his brother, Rich, at the farm where he worked. Rich and his boss, Kevin, were sitting at the table having a dish of ice cream before going out to start milking. Kevin took the call. After hanging up, he told Rich that he needed to go home immediately. He didn't tell him why; he just said to go home. Rich had no idea what he was coming home to. He told us later that he thought that his Camaro had gotten hit by a wagon or something.

His Camaro was his baby. One night while I was at work, Peggy called me and said I would never guess what she had sitting in the middle of her kitchen. Rich was working on his car at the time, and he wanted to paint the motor. However, it was cold outside, and the motor needed to be in where it was warm. He asked Peggy if he could bring the motor into the house overnight and let it get warm so he could paint it the next day, and he promised he would have it out by morning. Sure enough, he took it out of the car and put it in a wheelbarrow. There it sat, in the middle of the kitchen …

Rich got home soon after John came out with the towels. I remember that Rich came through the barn and when he saw me, took the fastest route by jumping out the window. He immediately ran to us, crying and losing it.

Peggy tried to get him to settle down. She told Rich that she needed his help to keep me stable. Fortunately, Kevin had followed Rich home. He came around the end of the barn, saw what was happening, and told Rich to listen to his mom. Rich dropped to his knees, wrapped his arms around my legs, and just sat there until the EMTs arrived.

Since we lived in a rural farming town, the paramedics and emergency response team came from several surrounding areas. Because farming accidents are usually serious, emergency responders are called from all over, many driving themselves straight to the farm. It didn't seem like much time had passed before the EMTs arrived. One blessing was that the ambulance driver knew we had moved to a different farm. He shared with us that some of the others riding in the ambulance noticed that he had gone past the road that we used to live on and told him he passed our farm; he told them that we had moved. Looking back, I wonder what would have happened if they had gone to the old farm first and not found us right away. Once again, God was watching over me.

It was interesting to me that, as each of the paramedics came running around the side of the wagon, they all asked if I was tangled up in the power takeoff shaft. I guess it looked like that because of how I was sitting on the shaft, and a lot of farm accidents do involve the power takeoff. One of the EMTs even called a local welding shop to come with a cutting torch to cut me out. Luckily, we didn't need it.

As the paramedics started working on me, they had a hard time getting the tape to stick to my body. I was starting to go into shock, and it began to rain. To make matters worse, it was a new ambulance, and they didn't have enough gauze to cover all of my injuries. They called Luther Hospital in Eau Claire to have them send Mayo One, the flight ambulance, to the farm to pick me up. Unfortunately, it was storming there, and they couldn't lift off from the pad.

The time came for them to put me on the stretcher. This was a bit of a problem also. First of all, when they laid me out, it opened up the big cavity the auger made in my stomach. That was the first pain that I remember having, and let me tell you—I've never forgotten it. I think this was when reality started to set in, and I started realizing how bad my injuries actually were. Earlier, I thought I would probably be in the hospital for a few days and then be right back to work. Now, I didn't even know if I'd make it to the hospital, and I definitely didn't know that the biggest fight was still to come.

When the EMTs attempted to put me on the stretcher, they had trouble getting me all of the way on. They tried to slide me down, but the whole pad slid down with me. They had to pick me up and slide the pad back into place. I guess I still had the presence of mind to be concerned about the mess I was making. The next thing I remember was apologizing to them as they put me in the ambulance. I had my boots on, and I was getting their new ambulance all dirty. They assured me that it was fine. I might have been dying, but at least I still had my sense of humor.

Peggy quickly called her mom and asked if her step-dad, Dave, and his boys could come do the chores. All she said was Dennis was in a bad accident and she didn't know if he was going to live. She hung up, not waiting for an answer.

Later, Grandma Pat called Dan and Amy's home in Nebraska and told Amy to go to meet Dan at work and then call her back. Once they found out what happened, they drove straight back to Wisconsin.

Peggy then asked if she could ride in the ambulance with me. They told her it would be best if she didn't. The driver later told her that they didn't want her in the ambulance because they didn't think that I would even make it to the hospital alive. Since they wouldn't allow her to ride with me, she asked if someone at the farm could give her a ride. Rich and John just looked at her, thinking she was going to make them stay home and do the milking. She told them that they could go with her, but none of them were going to drive. She knew if she drove, they would want her to go too fast. But if they drove, they would go too fast. Thankfully, Roger, our town chairman and emergency response team member, was there; he offered to take them to town.

Driving the country roads, Roger was driving pretty fast. When he got out to the main road heading into town, he slowed down and drove the speed limit. Rich was sitting behind him. Apparently, when Roger slowed down, Rich leaned over the front seat, got into Roger's face, and asked what the problem was.

Roger asked what he meant. Rich said to him, "Back on the side roads, you were in a hurry; but now you've slowed down." Roger told Rich that he thought it would be best if they would let the ambulance get to the hospital first so the doctors could get started working on his dad. Rich sat back and stopped arguing.

The driver of the ambulance, Aaron, told me later that as he drove through town, he had to go over a bump in the road. When he did, he heard me moan loudly. He also told me that every time he goes over that same spot, he remembers that day.

I was also told later that three men—Dale, Don, and Vern—came to the farm to work on the wagon. Dale is a good friend, and we used to work together. Don is my son-in-law's dad, and Vern is a neighbor and good friend. They took the wagon out to the pasture and shoveled all the hay out. Then, they took it to the barn to clean and wash it. When I spoke with Dale later, he shared with me that he sat in his office the next day, thinking about my accident. He told us that as he sat there, he started to get sick; there was so much of me on that wagon, he felt there was no way I could live.

Dale, Don, and Vern also told us that they found the reason the augers stopped turning—the main drive chain that runs the augers had broken. The size of a chain is based on a number system; the larger the number is, the bigger the chain. The main drive chain was a number 50, so it was fairly large. There is *no way* that my body could have broken that chain. When we heard why the augers stopped, we knew that it was God who broke that chain.

We are so thankful to all the paramedics, as well as these guys, for the part they played that day. More importantly, I am thankful for the love and mercy God showed me. Whether or not I lived, I knew something inside me had started to change ... but I still had a long way to go.

During this time, Peggy kept a journal of the events surrounding my accident and recovery. Some of it is a repeat, but I thought it would be good to see things from her perspective throughout the story. After all, she was suffering as much as I was.

Tuesday, June 9th

About 4:50 pm, Dennis got caught in the chopper box while unloading the haylage into the silo. John heard Den calling for help and went running from the pasture to see what was wrong. When John got to his dad, Den told him to shut off the power takeoff, help him down from the front of the wagon, and go call 911.

After John got me from the house, he grabbed some towels. When John came back with the towels, Den told us where he wanted them. He refused to move his left arm from his stomach. Even when I wanted to put a towel on the front of him, he said, "I need my arm right here." When Richard got to us, he held Den from the front, and I held him from the back. John was trying very hard to get a hold of Grandma and Grandpa Robinson and Grandma and Grandpa Hutchison, but no one was answering.

Dennis talked a little with the boys as they held one another. I told him not to talk too much to save his strength. He looked really bad. We didn't know if his organs were affected or if he was bleeding inside. We saw very little blood dripping from him, considering his injuries. His neck was cut on the left side that lay open, but it wasn't bleeding. His right arm and side also had cuts that looked deep. His left leg also had a small cut. The left side of his lower stomach was the worst. We saw a lot of haylage mixed with flesh sticking out of his stomach, but there wasn't a lot of blood.

Kevin Rosski, Richard's boss, came right after Richard. Rich kind of lost it for a moment, but we told him he needed to be strong for Dad, and he really did a wonderful job keeping Den from falling off the takeoff until the paramedics got there.

Mr. Amdall was the next one at the scene. He told the paramedics where we were, and then things started to fly. They took the towels away and tried to put bandages over the wounds, but the tape didn't want to stick. The one lady said, "Call and get the helicopter to the Barron site." They put him on oxygen right away as well.

Den told us he couldn't hold himself any longer and that he was going down, so they tried to get him on the stretcher. That was difficult because of the way the tractors and wagon were parked. There wasn't a lot of room for them to work.

Dennis asked Rich to hold him one last time before he died. He also told Rich he knew that he wasn't going to make it to Barron, he loved us, and he was so sorry. I told Dennis that God was going to take care of him and he was going to be okay because God knows how much we need him. We all just prayed while the paramedics were working on him.

Mr. Amdall gave the boys and me a ride to Barron. We prayed the Lord would keep Dennis strong and save him.

"Wow! Look at that Herd of People!"

The first hospital I was in that night was in my hometown: Barron, Wisconsin, about 15 miles from our farm. I don't remember much while being in the hospital, but I do remember my pastor coming into the emergency room and praying with me. I also remember Peggy being there.

But the one thing that really sticks out in my mind was seeing my dad standing over by the wall as the doctors were working on me. I looked at him and started crying. I also said to him, "I'm sorry." I don't know why I said that, but I did. It was probably because I started realizing what I had been putting my family through. Another thing I remember is an awful feeling that suddenly went through my body as I was lying on the table. I yelled, "What was that?" They told me they had just put a catheter in me, and they apologized for not letting me know what they were doing.

Our small hospital knew they couldn't take care of my long-term recovery. Once again, they called the hospital in Eau Claire to see if they could bring their helicopter to Barron to take me to their bigger hospital. The weather was getting worse in Eau Claire, however. There was no way the helicopter would be able to fly. The last thing I remember as they loaded me into the ambulance to drive me to Eau Claire was seeing Peggy and the boys standing in the ambulance port watching me leave. I wondered if I would ever see them again. The ambulance drove me to Luther Hospital in Eau Claire, Wisconsin, about 40 miles south of Barron; it is part of the Mayo Health System.

Because they started me on antibiotics and pain killers at this time, I have little to no recollection of what happened from this point forward. I can only share what Peggy and the rest of my family told me.

When we got to Barron, several friends and family members were already there. They let me go in to see Den, but he was really in a lot of pain. I told them to do whatever they needed, and I would be right outside.

They said every minute was important, so they sent him by ambulance to Eau Claire. They told us not to hurry because he would most likely be in surgery when we got there. The boys and I were all in farm clothes still, so we stopped to change before heading to Eau Claire. I borrowed a pair of Mom Robinson's shoes since mine had manure on them, and the boys borrowed clothes from their cousins. I rode to Eau Claire with Debbie, Kevin, Dad Robinson, and Rich. John rode with Aunt Pam and Tim. Several other friends and family members made the trip as well.

My mom made it to Luther even before I did. She happened to already be in Eau Claire giving blood at the Red Cross Blood Bank. Her blood type is O positive, and her blood was in big demand. When she arrived at the blood bank, there was a message for her saying there had been a farming accident and she needed to get to the hospital as soon as possible. They didn't tell her who it was, but she assumed it was me (this wasn't my first rodeo). Unfortunately, she had to drive all the way across town in order to get there.

As she was driving, she prayed for two things. The first was that all of the stoplights on the way to the hospital would be green. The second thing she prayed for was that I would not lose a limb. She thought for sure that was what had happened. By the time she arrived at the hospital, she knew at the very least, her first prayer was answered. The lights were all green as she drove through town.

I finally arrived in Eau Claire, and the doctors began to work on me immediately. As I was being worked on, more of our family and friends drove to Eau Claire to be with our family. When the doctor finally came in to speak with Peggy, he was shocked by the number of people there. Peggy wanted everyone to hear what the doctors thought needed to be done. The doctor told them they could stabilize me for the meantime, but they did not have the resources to take care of the long-term problems I was going to have. They made the decision to send me on to

St. Mary's Hospital in Rochester, Minnesota, the home of the Mayo Health System.

Since the weather had not improved, they called St. Mary's in Rochester and asked them to bring their bigger helicopter to Eau Claire. Because of the bad weather, they had to land at the airport instead of the hospital. An ambulance took the helicopter crew to the hospital to speak with the doctors so they could better understand my condition. In the meantime, the doctors were letting family come in a couple at a time to see me while Peggy was at my side. As I mentioned, I was out of it partly because of the pain killers, so my memories are somewhat spotty.

Apparently, my sense of humor was still intact. When Peggy's dad and step-mom came in to see me, I guess I asked them if any of their tomatoes had frozen off the night before. We had had a very rare June frost, and they had over 150 tomato plants that they were selling. When they told us they were able to save all the plants, I just said, "Rats!" I do *not* like tomatoes at all, but I *love* ketchup—go figure.

My sister Debbie and her husband, Kevin, came in to see me as well. Their second son, Daniel, was with them.

I think he was twelve at the time. Daniel loved coming out to the farm and staying a week or two at a time. If he had his choice, he probably never would have left. He knew that when there was work to be done, he had to get busy. But he also knew when the work was finished; he and the boys could play. During one stay at the farm, Debbie came to pick him up. He did not want to go, and he started crying and pitched a fit. I told him if he was going to act like that, he was not welcome at our house. I told him he should go home now and come back again if he wanted to. That did the trick; and sure enough, he was back at the farm as soon as his mom would let him. When they came in the room to see me, I guess I started in on Daniel, saying, "Now do you see why I tell you that you have to be careful on the farm? I don't want something like this to happen to you!" I guess poor Daniel just started crying. I'm sorry, Daniel; like I said before, I was in la-la-land.

The doctor told us that from what they could see, Den would need to be sent where there was better equipment to handle his surgeries down the road. They decided to transfer him, the next day, to St. Mary's Hospital in Rochester, better known as the "Mayo Clinic."

I do remember as I was being loaded into the ambulance, one crew member from the helicopter said, "Wow! Look at that herd of people!" Then he said, "I guess I shouldn't call them a herd because it makes them sound like a bunch of cows." Well, I was a dairy farmer ... I was told later that there was between 45 and 50 of our family and friends that had driven to Eau Claire to be with my family. It was most definitely a herd.

The next thing I remember was arriving at the airport and how it was such a tight fit loading the gurney into the helicopter. Then I heard the crew saying we had arrived in Rochester. It seemed like only a few minutes had passed. I spent that whole night in surgery.

Dad Hutchison and Sue took John and his cousin Daniel. Dad and Mom Robinson took Debby, Richard, and me. We met Travis

(Richard's best friend) along the way, so he, Rich, and his cousin David rode together to Rochester. When we arrived at Rochester, Den had been in surgery for about five minutes, so we waited and waited.

Between five and five-thirty the next morning, the trauma surgeon came out and spoke with Peggy and the rest of our family. She asked Peggy for her permission to do a tracheotomy on me. They felt that giving me a tracheotomy would be better than putting a tube down my throat all the time for the several additional surgeries I would need down the road.

Shortly after, another doctor came out to talk with Peggy. He said he was compelled to tell her that everyone needed to pray that I didn't get infection in any of my wounds. Peggy told him they had all been praying at the hospital, and there were people all over that were praying. The doctor told her, "I don't think you understand. If Dennis gets an infection, there is nothing we can do." Peggy told him she knew that each hospital I was in the night before had given me large doses of antibiotics. She said she was sure that they did the same thing here. Then, she asked what would happen if I did get an infection. The doctor told her that they usually cut the infected area away. Peggy had caught the word *usually*. She asked the doctor what he meant by that. He told her that my case was different. There was absolutely nothing left to cut away. I had been cut down to my main organs and ribs. There was nothing they could do should an infection set in.

She Literally Knows me Inside and Out.

*F*or the next seven days, the doctors had me in a chemi-
cally-induced coma, so I would lie still and my body could
start healing. Talk about a weird feeling—I woke up to find
out that I missed an entire week of my life!

During that week, several people came to the hospital
to be with my family. Dan and Amy arrived at the hospital
on Wednesday afternoon. Dan was only able to stay for
a week before he had to drive back to Nebraska and get
back to work, but Amy was able to stay an extra week to
be with us at the hospital. Her in-laws then paid her way
to fly home.

My older brother Don, his wife Peggy, and their family
were able to come up from Florida to see me that first week.

Unfortunately, I do not remember them being there. (It's been a real treat having two women named Peggy Robinson in our family.) Though I wasn't awake to visit with them, I know it was a blessing to my wife.

Visitors were always a helpful distraction for her and my family while I was in the coma. Sometimes these distractions even turned into adventures. While Amy was still with us at the hospital, she and Peggy decided that they would walk to K-Mart. Unfortunately, it was about a three-mile walk each way. The problem started when they came out from the store and it began to storm. Peggy didn't know how they would get back to the hospital without getting soaked. Amy decided that they would just have to call for a cab. And let me tell you—we country-folk don't get to see cabs very often! It was quite the experience for them, as neither of them had ridden in a taxi before. As Peggy would say: "We made memories."

While I was in the hospital, the farming back home could not stop. There were still cows to be milked and hay to be harvested and stored before it got too ripe. You would not believe the shock we felt when we heard that the farming community came together to put the last 100 acres of hay up for us!

Word had gotten out that they would start cutting hay on Monday—less than a week after my accident. Food started showing up immediately at the farm to feed the workers. In fact, Grandma Pat told us that she had been sitting out on the porch one morning, and she stepped into the house for a few minutes. When she went back outside, there were twelve packs of soda pop on the porch; someone brought them in for the workers.

Monday dawned bright and sunny, and ten of our neighbors arrived at our farm with their equipment to cut the hay. With so many hands, it only took a few hours to get it down. On Tuesday, three farmers brought their choppers and many other farmers brought their own wagons to bring the hay in. Richard's boss, Kevin, brought his blower for unloading the wagons. Ours was not very good, and it would not have kept up with the speed they needed to unload the hay and keep up with the choppers.

At one point, they had wagons lined up from behind the barn all the way out the driveway and out onto the road. That would have been a sight to see! Before long, the silo was full, and there were still nine wagons loaded with hay. They put that hay in a silo that we usually use for corn. There was still hay on the ground too!

The next day, five neighbors brought their balers to our farm and baled the rest of the hay. That day, they baled 60 big, round bales and 2,700 small, square bales of hay. Then the farmers used a conveyer belt to send the square bales to a hay loft in the barn. We only had one conveyer, so someone brought another conveyer over to help get the hay up faster. One of our neighbors wanted to buy some hay from us, so they even loaded bales into his barn!

It was amazing to hear how our community came together to help us, but it was even better to watch it all happening. Our son-in-law's sister, Michelle, was there all three days and recorded a lot of it on video. We were able to watch it when we got home. It brought tears to my eyes, when I saw what they did for us. I truly believe the Lord used these people to bless our family. Though we could never repay them for what they did, we later had the opportunity to thank them properly. I'll get to that in a bit.

Monday, June 15

Dennis slept a lot today. He is very tired from all the visitors. So many family members have come to visit this past week. The doctors are washing Den twice a day around 8:00 in the morning and 8:00 at night. So far there is no infection. Praise the Lord! They started to sew up some of the wounds and put drains in each of them. Den is wondering if his right arm is finished. The doctor says that if there is no infection, it should heal okay. The doctor took out a couple of the IV shunts today. They had put extra ones in just in case they needed them.

I was told there were 10 men with hay cutters at our farm today. They put our hay down in about 2½ hours. That must have been something to see!

While in the coma, one of the first things they had to do was tie restraints around my wrists. They did not want me to start digging at my injuries. I guess I fooled them. Peggy told me that when she and my surgeon would stand in my intensive care room talking, I would work the restraints up to my elbows. Then I would bend my arms and pull at the tubes and bandages. The doctor said to Peggy, "Look at him. I have never seen such a desire to live." When the restraints didn't work, the next thing they tried was to put mittens on my hands so I couldn't grab the tubes and pull them out. Peggy told me she even had to sweet-talk me into pulling my fingers together. I was spreading them out to keep them from getting the mittens on. I guess I was a fighter!

One of the first things that I remember after waking up from the coma was realizing I was unable to talk because the doctors had done a tracheotomy on me. The first question they asked me was, "Do you know where you are?" I got that one wrong. For some reason, I had it in my head that I was in the Twin Cities (Minneapolis/St. Paul, Minnesota). What a surprise to find out that I was at the St. Mary's Hospital (Mayo Clinic) in Rochester!

Because I couldn't talk, I had to write my answers down on paper every time someone asked me a question.

I absolutely *hated* having to do that. First of all, I am the world's worst speller. Secondly, I would only get a couple letters written down before they started guessing what I was trying to tell them—talk about frustrating!

Not only was having the tracheotomy annoying because I couldn't talk, but I very much disliked having my tracheotomy cleaned. The nurse would stick something in the tracheotomy to make me cough. Then, they would take a suction hose and suck out any phlegm or junk that was built-up in there. I knew it was helping me, but what a terrible feeling!

Tuesday, June 16

It's been one week since the accident. Today, the doctor said they were going to plug the tracheotomy, but the one Den has can't be plugged. He has to wait ten days before they can put another one in. They also said they want him to sit up for a while. The doctor is cutting back on the morphine from 3 to 2 this afternoon.

*They are also going to cut back on the feeding
tube. They gave him a fan in his room today
to try to cool him down. David, Den's brother,
called to check on him as well. He said that they
made it back to New York in record time.*

*We have met some very nice people here
in the ICU. One man named Allen had a tree
branch come around and hit him in the stomach
while they were pulling it with a tractor. It looks
like he will have a long road ahead of him too.
We went down to the chapel today to pray with
Allen's sister, mother, and girlfriend.*

While I was in the ICU, it was always very special
to be able to have visitors come in and see me. (It was
a two-and-a-half hour drive from my hometown for them
just to get here.) During one of those visits, on Father's
Day, we found out that one of the elderly men from our
home church had passed away. I did not know him really
well; but after being as close to death as I was, it had taken

on a whole new meaning. I realized how permanent death really is—you don't get another chance.

My Uncle Orville and Aunt Bonita also came to see me while I was in the ICU. They brought Grandma Robinson to see me—she was in her nineties at the time. Unfortunately, they came during a terrible storm. During the month of June, there were more storms and tornadoes in Rochester than I remember ever seeing. It seemed like we had a tornado go through town every week that I was there. One of the worst storms happened to be while Grandma Robinson was there. They made all of the visitors go down to the basement, and they put all of the patients in the hallway. There was always something eventful going on during my hospital stay!

Wednesday, June 17

Den's been wide awake since 3:00 this morning. The doctor came around 5:00 and said that he's doing great. He's been running a 101.2 temperature for a while now. He's always hot, but still no infection. He feels bloated, and his stomach hurts a lot, but he is still doing well.

This afternoon, Den woke up and said he needed the bed pan, so I went and got the nurse. When she came in, Den wanted to know what was wrong. I told him that he said he needed the bed pan. Apparently, Den was dreaming and didn't really need it. The nurse said it was fine because she only charges a quarter a time. She said she hoped to make a little money this evening. Ha! The nurses and staff are so kind to us.

The doctor did a throat test on Den to see how well he could swallow. Den did well, so they allowed him to have some chicken broth, lemon ice, and orange juice for dinner. He didn't eat a lot, but he said it tasted good. It's hard for him to use his right arm, so I fed him..

There are so many people hurting here. We've seen some lose their battle with life, and others have won and gone home. Life sure is short.

I'm told that our neighbors have been chopping our hay and filling our silo and hay loft. The boys even raised the unloader in the small silo so they could run the hay in there. Everyone says the boys are doing a super job at home. Patty and Dave are doing the apartments for me right now. Praise the Lord for family and friends!

At this point, I think it's important to share what some of my injuries were. I had a large cut on my right side where the augers tore my side open. The remaining scar is about 15 inches long and 1 ½ inches wide at the widest point. On my right arm, just below the elbow, I had a cut across the arm that was 3 to 4 inches long. I remember looking at the cut and thinking that I wouldn't be able to use my right arm anymore. I just knew I would never be able to work again. For a workaholic like me, this seemed like the end of the world.

The augers also cut the left side of my neck open. The largest injury was the open cavity on the left side of my stomach. When I arrived at the hospital, it was a mess. In fact, one of the doctors that first worked on me at the hospital in Barron told me later that he remembered me because he basically dug a bale of hay out of my stomach. This cavity was the biggest concern for infection since the auger cut down to my vital organs and ribs.

Thursday, June 18

Den got up in the chair for about an hour today. He slept pretty good last night because they gave him some sleeping medicine. His big wound is really hurting today, and the morphine isn't helping. It sounds like the doctors are going to change medications for him to see if that will help. The physical therapist came in today and did exercises with Den around 2:30 as well.

Bruce and Donna (Dan and Amy's boss from Nebraska) called a pastor friend from Rochester and asked him to come and check on Den. He was a very nice man. He said if we didn't mind, he would stop and check in on Den again later.

Den waited 2½ hours today to have a doctor come and give him something for pain. When they came, they opened Den's wounds and pushed on his stomach. They gave him two more kinds of medication and said they would keep watching his sores really close, but at this point, everything looked pretty good.

Pam, Jeff, and Tim came to the hospital today and took me out for dinner while Den was sleeping. When we got back, we noticed a huge change in Dennis. The doctor had changed the tracheotomy and Den has an air mask. He can talk now too.

After Amy, Pam, Jeff, and Tim left, I noticed I must have left my purse at the restaurant, so I called there. When they said they couldn't find it, I felt sick. When I went into Den's room to tell him, I saw it there on the floor. What a relief.

Beginning with my first day of recovery, I was taken twice a day to the shower cart. They would come get me from my room and put me on a stainless steel table that they had *obviously* just pulled out of the freezer because it was *so* cold. Then they would take me to a room down the hall where they did what they call a "debridement." They would wash out the big, open cavity in my stomach with something like a mini pressure-washer in order to remove any hay left inside me. Once they finished, they would pack my stomach with gauze, which served two purposes: first, the gauze helped grab hold of foreign objects in my stomach; second, it allowed my stomach to heal from the inside out.

The first few times I had to go to the shower cart, they put me to sleep. Eventually, they did it while I was awake. They had me push my morphine button ahead of time so I would not be in a lot of pain. But I do remember that there was one spot that just about sent me off the table every time they hit it with water. They told me it was probably an exposed nerve ending that was very tender when the water hit it—whatever it was, it *wasn't* fun.

For the sake of my manhood; I shouldn't share this, but I am going to anyway. One day, as they were doing the shower cart thing, the nurses asked if I would like to have my hair washed. I couldn't remember the last time it had been washed, so I said, "Sure." A while back, there was a commercial for Calgon, the bath crystals for women. In the commercial, they would show a beautiful woman taking a bath. She would be lost in the moment, and she would say "Calgon, take me away!"

Well, I guess I got lost in the moment too. As they were washing my hair, I said out loud, "Calgon, take me away!" They said, "What?!" I had to explain to them that it was a joke between Peggy and me. If something felt really good—such as a shower or a back rub or anything like that—we would say to each other, "Calgon, take me away!" Needless to say, that was the talk around the intensive care unit for the day.

Friday, June 19

When I came in to check on Dennis at 2:30 this morning, I was shocked to see Aunt Donna sitting in his room. She apparently drove through the night to get there after she got off work. Around 5:00, the doctors came and told us the "bigwigs" would come in tonight to see what they thought about Dennis' wounds. During his shower cart this morning, the "top dog" doctor went in to check on Den. He said his wounds look good. Another tornado came through Rochester today. Dad said they got 2¼ inches of rain overnight.

Instead of sewing the large cut on my arm shut, they just put a big stitch on each end of it and washed it out while I was in the shower cart—twice a day every day. It's amazing how the body works. Even though it was such a long, deep cut, it eventually healed and closed on its own.

Saturday, June 20

There were a bunch of rowdy kids on our floor in the middle of the night. Thankfully, they are gone now, and Den was able to sleep through it. The doctor took Den's face mask off this morning, and now he only has the oxygen tube under his nose.

Den sat up about 7 hours today. He ate a little potato soup and ice cream. He also drank some grape juice. There were many visitors at the hospital today as well.

I can also remember meeting my trauma surgeon for the first time—the one that put me back together. She was a short lady, younger than me. She was from Puerto Rico, and I had a bit of a hard time understanding her. She came into my ICU room and introduced herself. Then, she asked if it would be okay for her to bring some of her interns into my room. She wanted them to see what was going on with me. I nodded that it would be fine, but I was shocked when nine people walked in behind her! I thought, "Come on in! Enjoy the show!" Even then, the whole staff was very impressive—from the top doctors all the way down to the cleaning people. They all had a servant's heart and went well out of their way to make all of us comfortable.

Sunday, June 21

Today is Father's Day. We have so much to be thankful for! They took out some more IV ports today. They have also stopped the morphine drip, and Den is off the oxygen tab.

They brought cereal, eggs, juice, and milk for breakfast. We were able to push Den in a wheel chair to the big waiting room this afternoon, but he tired fast, so it was a short visit. He had a lot of visitors again today. Autumn even stayed the night with me.

Monday, June 22

The doctor took out every other stitch on Dennis' neck and right side. They also pulled his catheter. They said they want us to learn how to wash his stomach wound, depending on how much pain Den can stand when being washed out. Not sure exactly what the doctor is thinking or when we'll start that. The doctors also want all dirt and oil off Den's hands and nails. They fear it could cause some problems with infection. Den walked about twelve yards today with the walker. He did really well!

The third week I was in Rochester, I was taken out of the ICU and put in a general-care room. This was a huge blessing because I could then have more visitors. During one such visit, while we were talking with two couples from our church, I received a phone call from my brother Dave.

Dave and his family were living in upstate New York at the time. He had come to Rochester to see me during the week that I was in the coma. His brother-in-law died from cancer the same day as my accident. I wish I could have been able to talk to Dave at the time.

It was great to hear Dave's voice, even if it was over the phone. We talked for a few minutes, and then he shared with me a conversation he had with a gentleman from the church he and his family attended. Dave had shared with his church family about my accident, and he had asked for them to pray for me. A farmer in the church told Dave he kind of knew what I was going through. Dave told me he looked at the man, wondering how he could possibly know what I was going through. The farmer shared that he had a sixteen-year-old young man helping on his farm one summer.

The day before, they had been unloading a chopper box, something like what I had been pulled into. Because they had filled the silo, they were not able to get everything off of the wagon. The silo would have settled overnight, so they planned to finish unloading the wagon that day. The farmer had to go to town for a meeting, so it was one of the young man's chores for the day. The farmer then shared with Dave that all of a sudden, the dog ran up to the house and started barking. Because this was unusual for their dog, his wife went out to see what was going on. What she found, as she followed their dog, was the young man's sweatshirt wrapped around the augers on the chopper box. Apparently, he decided to crawl into the box to clean it out while it was still running. He got tangled up in the augers, pulled into the blower, and lost his life.

As Dave was telling me this, I started to bawl. I told him that was one of the thoughts that had gone through my mind. The two couples that were there talking with Peggy as I was on the phone looked at me, wondering what was going on. After I got off of the phone with Dave, I shared with them the story he had relayed. It was an affirmation of what God had done for me. I knew that I shouldn't be alive. *He* broke the chain that day. God gave me another chance to get my heart right with Him the day of the accident, and I have worked at keeping my heart right every day since.

Tuesday, June 23

Den had a bad cough this morning that wouldn't leave him. A doctor from the respiratory department came by and listened to Den's chest. He said it sounded like the start of a collapsed lung or fluid on the lung. Den threw up, so they had to do suction on his tracheotomy. After that, he felt a lot better.

The doctor asked how his leg felt; he said it was tender in the calf area. The doctor said that's a sign of blood clots, so Den needed to sit up longer and walk as much as he could to prevent them.

A lady from our church came to visit today. She brought an envelope that had $400 in it. What a blessing! It will come in very handy for meals and supplies.

Wednesday, June 24

The doctor today said Den's wounds are looking good, but his cultures came back positive. We have to wear gowns, gloves, and masks. Den also got moved today to the second floor. I had to make four trips to 7th floor to get all of my things.

Dave called from New York and told Den about a 16-year-old boy who had a farm accident like Den. He got hurt on a chopper box too. Den started crying while Dave told him the story. Den said those very thoughts went through his mind during his accident.

Tonight I had to sleep with a gown, mask, and gloves on. At 9:45, the nurse came in and told me to get in the bathroom. They pushed Dennis' bed up next to the bathroom because we had another tornado warning. It lasted about an hour.

The next major step on the road to recovery was having the hole in my stomach covered. I was moved to a different floor in order to prepare for the repair. The day of my surgery, the surgeon came in and told us what he would do and what to expect during the recovery time. He told me they were going to do a skin graft, and the donor site (the place where they would borrow the skin) would hurt. He told me it would feel like I was playing ball and slid into home base wearing shorts. But what he forgot to tell me was that I was playing on blacktop!

He also shared that once the skin graft was complete, I would have to lie still with my body slightly elevated for five days. He told me there would probably be other doctors coming in wanting to look at the skin graft. I was told to *not* let them take the bandages off. The surgeon then proceeded to roll me down to the surgical waiting room. I was impressed that he would take the time to personally do that.

The next thing I remember after being taken to surgery was waking up in the recovery room. The pain I felt was unbearable. They had taken two pieces of skin off my right thigh. Then, they sent it through a machine that stretched it so it could cover four times the area that it would normally cover. It felt like my right leg was on fire! Thankfully, they knocked me out for a while so I would not be in so much pain.

Thursday, June 25

The doctor came to check on Dennis this morning and said he was going to bring the plastic surgeon by to see if Den was ready for surgery. He said they would try to do the skin graft on Tuesday. He also said Den would probably be in the hospital at least two more weeks, maybe even longer.

I washed laundry today. When I got back, there were two families from our church visiting Den. While they were there, the nurse came in and moved Dennis to a bigger room; one with a shower and a cot for me to sleep on.

Dennis is really improving. The doctor took out the stitches from his neck and right side. He also pulled the drains from Den's left side. He had his first shower sitting on a stool today. The white collar holding his tracheotomy got wet, so they took it off. Den coughed, and his tracheotomy plug shot out of the hole in his neck, and they had to put it back in. They also changed his tracheotomy collar support.

Peggy was at my side during the entire process. Because she could handle it, being the farm girl that she was, they allowed her to watch when they worked on me. She had the opportunity to see my open wound as well as what was going on inside me. I love telling people that she is the one woman who literally knows her husband inside and out!

An important moment during my recovery was when Peggy was able to give me a haircut. She asked the nurses for permission, and they said she could do it as long as she kept the hair out of my wounds. Ever since we have been married, she has been the only one to cut my hair. A haircut might not seem like a big deal, but it meant something to us that day as we "made another memory."

It was a good thing I left my grooming to someone who knew me. Peggy shared with me that the doctors talked about shaving my beard off while I was still in the ICU. Now, I've had a beard for over 20 years, and I tell you what—if they would have done that I would *not* have been a happy camper!

Friday, June 26

The doctors told Den today that he could eat anything he wanted now—even food from home! James, one of Den's nurses, told us that he had seen a lot of things while working at the hospital, but this case was right near the top of the difficult things he's had to work with.

Saturday, June 27

Tonight the lights went out at 8:11 and didn't return until 8:55. Even then, they only came back on because of the generators. Apparently, the whole city of Rochester is out of power. They said it could be Monday before the power is turned back on. We understand one of the main power lines broke and fell into a flooded area, and no one can get to where the line is right now.

Uncle John and Aunt Beryl came today, and we spent several hours in the dark with them. The nurses moved us into the hallway and gave us flashlights. They said ten miles north of us, there were a lot of trees fallen on homes and cars because of yet another tornado.

The next five days were some of the hardest I had in the hospital. It was so difficult to just lie there for five days. I wasn't allowed to move an inch. It was also tough because

Peggy had to go home and take care of some business with the farm and the apartments. She was gone for two days and nights—they were very possibly the longest days of my life.

Peggy is my soul mate. I love her very much. My dad had come to see me in the hospital, and he gave Peggy a ride home. While on the way home, Dad and Peggy were talking, and she reminded him about a comment he made many years ago. We had been at a church meeting, and we were goofing off a little. Dad made the comment, "Good thing you two married each other. You saved two other people a lot of misery." Poor Dad; he doesn't remember saying it, but I heard it. Of course, we didn't mind. In the years since the accident, we have grown so close to each other. In fact, we are closer in our marriage now than we have ever been. Like Peggy says, "If this is misery, bring it on!"

As I said earlier, those were two of the longest days of my life—not having Peggy by my side. John was there, but I'm sure you know how hard it is to keep a sixteen-year-old tied down to one spot. After all, there was a large hospital to explore! In fact, we were told that there are 36 miles of hallway at St. Mary's Hospital and he wanted to see it all.

Wednesday, July 1

I just returned to Rochester after going home for a couple of days. Dennis sure was glad to see me. He wants to go home, but I told him we had to be patient. I reminded him of the saying, "Be patient; God isn't finished with me yet."

One of the five days I had to stay in bed, Peggy was feeding me supper. Of course, she *had* to take advantage of the fact that I wasn't allowed to move, so she had a little fun. She took a fork full of food and pretended that it was an airplane. She flew it through the air and said, "Open your mouth! Here comes the plane of food!" That certainly did *not* make my day.

People talk about the power of advertising. Well, I experienced it firsthand. I cannot tell you how many times in a two or three day period that I saw a commercial for Pringles potato chips! Well, I eventually had to have some.

I finally sent Peggy out to go and find me a can. They tasted a whole lot better than hospital food!

The five days finally passed, and my plastic surgeon came in to take the bandage off my stomach. Sure enough, several doctors had come in, wanting to look at it. I told them to keep their distance if they valued their life. When he took the bandage off, I guess you could say I was surprised at what I saw. There were safety pins and rubber bands pulling everything together—talk about modern equipment!

The surgeon gave me permission to start getting up and trying to walk again. I was told that for every day someone is down, it takes at least three days to recover. That was *so* true. The first time I sat up, I thought I was going to throw up. My head started spinning, and I thought I was going to fall over. I had to lie down again before I ever got to my feet. It was a very slow process, and I'm pretty sure that God gave the physical therapists who worked with me an extra portion of patience. Over time, I was finally able to get to my feet and start walking. It was almost like having to learn how to walk all over again.

Saturday, July 4

No one came to visit today, but we've had lots of phone calls. We watched a couple of movies, and I read to him out of a book that Amy sent and then another one that Sue left here.

Once a day, the nurse came in and fixed the bandage on my leg where they took the skin graft, which was very painful. The bandage itself was a clear, thin plastic material that had sticky tape on all sides. The doctor said that where he had taken the skin off feels about the same as having a third-degree burn—I can attest to that. The area weeps a clear fluid of some kind. The nurses had to stick a needle in the plastic and draw out some of the fluid. Then, they had to put another clear bandage over the spot where they had drawn from. Eventually, there were so many patches on the main bandage that they had to take them all off and start over with a new one. Talk about painful! I can honestly say that these moments had to be the most painful parts of the whole recovery process.

Throughout my stay in the hospital, we received countless cards of encouragement. Of course, we received many of them from our friends and family, but someone had also put our name into an organization known as "Angel Tree." We received cards and letters from people all over the United States who we didn't even know. Included with each letter was some kind of little angel that they either made or purchased. These were so special to us. One family shared with us, through the Angel Tree, that they had lost a young son in a farming accident. They found through this experience that when a family goes through a tragedy, it would either make them bitter or it would make them better. They chose to become better through their tragedy. Well, I had tried the *bitter* side of life. It almost killed me on more than one occasion. I decided that I would try to make life *better* for me and my family.

Speaking of angels, I can remember lying in the ICU and thinking about a passage from the Bible that talked about God's angels watching over us. I asked Peggy if she could remember where to find it, but she said she couldn't. It wasn't but a day or two later that our pastor, Dennis

Pond, drove over to visit. He asked if he could read us a passage from the Bible. To our surprise, it was the very passage that I had been asking Peggy about! He read Psalm 91:11-12, 15-16: "For he shall give his angels charge over thee, to keep thee in all thy ways. They shall bear thee up in their hands, lest thou dash thy foot against a stone. He shall call upon me, and I will answer him: I will be with him in trouble: I will deliver him and honor him. With long life will I satisfy him, and show him my salvation." The day of the accident, June 9, 1998, I know God heard my call for help, and He had His angels watching over me. He saved me from certain death.

Scars are Sexy on a Man!

Though I knew God's hand was with me during this time, there was one thing that kept popping up in the back of my mind: I was glad to be alive, but what was I going to be good for? How would I provide for my family?

The day finally came when the doctors told us that we could go home. July 9th was the day. It was exactly one month after the accident. My mom and dad drove to Rochester to pick us up. That was a very special ride home.

The doctors decided to send me home with the tracheotomy still in, but they put a special plug in it so I could talk. Because they weren't sure what lay ahead in my recovery, they decided it would be best to have it there in case I needed future surgeries.

Having been indoors for a month made me look at things in a whole new light. Everything looked brighter—which makes sense after staring at hospital walls for a whole month. Arriving back at the farm was a special event. Our boys were there with our dog Seemore, a pure-bred Pekinese. We named him Seemore because when he was a puppy, his head seemed like it was nothing but eyes, thus he could "see more." Peggy's mom and step-dad were also there waiting for us. We can't thank Grandma Pat, Grandpa Dave, and our boys enough for keeping the farm going while we were gone. It looked even better when we got home than it did when we left.

Thursday, July 9

This is the day we have been waiting for. We are going home! Den had to go home in pajamas from the hospital because I hadn't brought him anything else to wear. The van was full of flowers, cards, and medical supplies.

He was tired and hurting, but Dennis made the trip. When we got home, our road had just been re-paved, making the last part of the trip extra smooth.

The farm looked great. They had been working very hard to clean everything up. Dennis is very weak, and we have to do everything for him, but we are so very thankful to have him home. We are thankful for the Lord's protection over the last month. I know we have a long road ahead of us still, but I am thankful that God will help us get through it.

It was so wonderful to be back in my own home. I couldn't wait to drink some of our own milk out of the bulk tank. This milk would still have the cream in it, so it would taste very rich. And what a feeling to be back in my own bed! Unfortunately, I couldn't take care of myself. I didn't realize it at the time, but there was still a long road ahead of me before I could do that. Feeding myself was about the only thing I *could* do.

My first week home didn't go the way I thought it would. I started getting sick with flu-like conditions. I couldn't eat, and all-around I just did not feel well. Between my accident and month-long stay at the hospital, I had lost 50 pounds. Now I'm a big guy, but 50 pounds is still a lot to lose. We figured that I lost another 10 pounds after going home. One night, Grandma Pat sat up in bed, realizing that it could have been the milk that was making me sick. The next morning, she called Peggy right away and told her not to give me any more milk from the tank. Sure enough, that did the trick; I started feeling much better after that.

Upon telling my trauma surgeon about it at our first visit, she explained that they had given me large amounts of antibiotics to fight the chance of infection. It killed not only the bad bacteria, but also the good bacteria as well. Talk about being frustrated! There was a tank full of milk just a few yards from the house, but we had to drive all the way into town to buy milk. I couldn't even enjoy the milk produced on my own farm! I think it was about a year before I was able to start drinking it again.

I was thankful to have the tracheotomy plug because I could talk and didn't have to answer questions on paper anymore or write to carry on a conversation. Also, now that I was home, I was able to have more visitors come and see me. I was also able to take more calls from friends and family. One such call came from Paul, Peggy's brother. I was resting in bed when he called, so Peggy brought me the phone. While we were talking, my tracheotomy plug fell out, and I couldn't speak at all. I tried to call out to Peggy for help, but nothing would come out. Somehow I got her attention, and she was able to find where the plug had landed, clean it up, and put it back in place. What a helpless feeling!

One day, our elderly neighbor came over to visit. He shared with us that he had gone to the clinic in Barron one day to get a shot of some kind. While he was waiting in the clinic, the hospital staff came in and told him, along with the other patients, that they would have to go home and come in another day. As it turned out, it was the day of my accident, and they were bringing me into the hospital. They wanted to have as many staff available as possible. He had no idea it was his own neighbor who had caused that to happen!

To make it easier for me to get in and out of bed, we added an extra mattress—but I still couldn't even do *that* without help! Even with the extra bed height, Peggy had to grab my legs with one hand and hold my back with the other hand to kind of pick me up and lay me down all at the same time. Thankfully, Peggy's mom came over every day to help take care of me so that Peggy could get the farming done. It was a huge help and blessing for Peggy, since she knew that I was being taken care of while she was working.

Our first visit back to Rochester quickly arrived, just one week after going home. As I said before, it is a 2½ hour drive each way to Rochester. The trauma surgeon almost immediately pulled the tracheotomy plug out; she said that we should not need it any more. Surprisingly, she did not stitch the opening shut. She explained that part of the body heals very quickly. (And it did! It closed less than a week later.) She told us she was happy with the progress of my recovery, but we would still have to come back for a few more visits.

While discussing the scars on my body, she made a comment that I *loved*, but Peggy just rolled her eyes. She told us if I would have been a woman, they would have had to do a lot more work on my stomach to make it look better. I would not have been able to wear a bikini without more cosmetic surgery. (Praise the Lord I'm not a woman!) She said since I was a man though, the scars were okay—scars are *sexy* on a man! Like I said, Peggy just rolled her eyes. I have had to remind Peggy how "sexy" my scars are every once and awhile.

Not long after returning home, we received our bill from the hospital. We were shocked by the size of it! It turned out to be 19 computer pages long. Out of curiosity, I always wanted to go through it to see how much morphine I had been given, but I never did.

The next few weeks went fairly well. The hardest part for me, though, was sitting in the house while everyone else was doing the farming I wanted to do. I started to get a little down and depressed. Grandma Pat was there helping take care of me, and she shared that I have a lot to be thankful for. First of all, I was alive. Secondly, I had a family that loved me very much. I also had friends and family that were willing to drop everything and come help us on the farm. Even knowing this, it was still hard to be out of the action. It took some time for me to realize that I was not all "washed up"—that there might be something out there that I could do.

Over the next few weeks, we noticed that it had started getting harder and harder for me to breathe. Five weeks after coming home from the hospital, we had an appointment with the plastic surgeon that had done the skin graft on my stomach. He looked at the progress of the healing and was pleased. I still had one of those clear bandages on my leg at this time. They took it off, and once again, it was *extremely* painful.

While talking with him, Peggy mentioned how I was struggling to breathe. He said that he had noticed it. Peggy asked if there was anyone we could see about it while we were there. The doctor made a call to the Respiratory Department. He was told there was no way we could be seen that day. They told us to go home, and they would send us an appointment card for when we could be seen. It felt great to be on the road to recovery. Little did we know there were more setbacks to come.

"The In-Flight Movie was Disappointing."

*W*ithin a day or two of returning home, we got an appointment card saying that my appointment would be in two weeks. I thought, "Seriously? I am having problems *breathing!* I have to wait two weeks to be seen?"

The next week was extremely tough, as it got harder and harder to breathe. Just about the only thing that helped was standing in the shower with the hot water running, so I did that often. The water bill was definitely high that month, but I was cleaner than I had been in years!

I woke up Sunday morning gasping for each breath of air I could get. We went to church anyway, and I must have sounded pretty bad. The couple that was sitting in front of us kept turning around and looking at me like, "Are you going to be okay?"

We made it through the service and went out to the car. Peggy begged me to let her take me to the hospital and have the doctor check me out. In my stubbornness, I told her, "I'll be fine!" I told her that we would call the Mayo Clinic the next morning and tell them what was happening. After all, they were the ones that had taken care of me up to this point.

Needless to say, she was not happy about waiting, but she headed for home anyway. When we got there, I was extremely tired and didn't feel like eating lunch. I tried to lie down for a while, but that made it harder to breathe. I finally had Peggy help me get up and into the shower; that had always seemed to do the trick before. While I was sitting in the shower, Peggy called her sister, Patty, and told her what was going on. She convinced Peggy that she needed to call the Barron Hospital right away. She did, and when she got done explaining what I was experiencing, they told her to get me to the hospital as fast as she could.

When Peggy got off the phone with them, she told me that I needed to get out of the shower—we were going for a little ride! I asked where we were going, and she told me that she had called the hospital. They were waiting for us to get there. Despite my stubbornness, I got dressed anyway, and we went on her "little ride." Apparently, when the hospital staff heard that Dennis Robinson was coming in, everyone started to scramble, remembering the last time I was there. I guess that's what happens when you live in a small town.

From the moment we arrived at the hospital, they started running all kinds of tests. I felt a bit like a lab rat. My blood oxygen was low, and my heart was beating much faster than it was supposed to be. They injected me with steroids to try to slow my heart rate, but that did not help at all. Then they put nitroglycerin under my tongue, but that only made me light-headed. They even did chest x-rays, but they still couldn't find what was causing the problem.

They finally decided to send us to the hospital in Eau Claire again. After making some calls, they told us that they were going to send us to Chippewa Falls instead.

Chippewa Falls is just shy of an hour from Barron, our hometown. They said that the two hospitals shared an Ear, Nose, and Throat specialist (ENT), and she was at the smaller hospital that day. There were four women in the ambulance with me: a nurse, the driver, and two interns.

When we were getting close to Chippewa Falls, the nurse got on the radio with the hospital to let them know my vitals and that we were about 10 minutes away. When she got off the radio, the driver asked her if she knew where the hospital was. Neither of them was used to going to the hospital in Chippewa Falls. Almost everyone they trans-ported was sent to Luther Hospital in Eau Claire since it was much bigger.

The nurse said that she didn't know where it was; she assumed that the driver would have gotten directions. As I overheard this conversation, I thought I would stick my two cents in. I asked the nurse why she didn't just get back on the radio and ask the hospital for directions. She got this look on her face and said that she didn't think that was a good idea. I thought to myself, "And they say *men* don't ask for directions." I guess I can't fault her; she didn't want to look dumb. Well, what were we going to do? Fortunately, Peggy and I used to live in the area while we were working for a local farmer, and we used to drive past the hospital every time we went to town. I wound up sitting up in the ambulance telling *them* where to go. Once we were in town, they were able to follow the "H" signs to the hospital.

When we arrived, the ENT examined me. She asked how long I had been having a hard time breathing. I told her that it had been coming on for about six weeks, but the last couple of weeks had been the worst. She asked why we didn't have it looked at before. I didn't really have a good answer for her except that I had mentioned it last time we were in Rochester. Then she said, "You farmers are all alike. You have to be on your death bed before you come in to see a doctor!" I had to raise my hand and say, "Guilty!"

She sprayed this awful-tasting stuff in my mouth to numb my throat. Then, she ran a fiber-optic device up my nose and down into my esophagus. She did this in both nostrils and even invited Peggy to take a look in there as well. (How romantic!) She said that she could only run the tube in as far as my vocal cords, or she would run the risk of damaging them. The doctor then proceeded to explain what she thought was going on. I likely had some scar tissue building up where the tracheotomy had been, which apparently is a common complication. She said on a rare occasion, some people have scar tissue build up all the way around the esophagus; she believed that was what happened to me. I would likely need laser surgery to take that portion of my esophagus out and then have it sewn back together. Since no one at that hospital was qualified to do such a delicate operation, I would need to go back to Rochester to have it done.

She immediately began the process of getting me transferred to the Mayo Clinic. Apparently, obstruction of the airway takes precedence over a lot of medical issues, so she decided to have me air-lifted out. She said that she would sleep better knowing I got there quickly. Once again, they called for the helicopter from Eau Claire, but it was already on the way to Rochester with someone else. They called Rochester directly to send their chopper instead.

This second ride was a little nicer—I actually remember it! I wasn't in la-la-land this time. When we landed at the hospital, one of the flight nurses asked what I thought of the flight. I told her that it was pretty neat, but I pointed to the monitor that was showing my vitals and said, "The in-flight movie was disappointing."

I was immediately taken to the emergency room to be examined. The doctor on call once again sprayed that awful-tasting junk in my mouth, and back up he went through both nostrils. When he was finished checking me, the doctor sent me to the intensive care unit. Talk about déjà vu! He told us that the head of the Ear, Nose, and Throat Department would come and take a look at me first thing in the morning. Thankfully, my folks once again drove Peggy to Rochester so that she could be with me.

About 2:00 in the morning, I started to cough and gag on some phlegm that was caught in my throat. The nurses came in, took a look at me, and called for the doctor from the ER to come immediately. They wheeled some carts into my room that looked like tool chests. For the life of me, I still don't know why! They must have had some medical things in them, but they never used them to help me. For a minute, I thought I might die; I was choking and gasping for air. When they all stepped out of the room, I finally coughed up a chunk of phlegm. That seemed to stop the choking for the time being. It was the most important "loogie" I've ever hocked up!

Early Monday morning, the head ENT specialist came to see me. If I remember right, he also had two or three interns with him as well. Once again, I was sprayed in my mouth, and then up both nostrils they went. I've told friends that it's no wonder my nose runs so much—considering how many times doctors went up in there!

He confirmed the first doctor's diagnosis of seeing a lot of scar tissue. He did mention, however, something about possibly seeing a foreign object. He went on to explain how the surgery would be done. In order to get to the area they needed to work on, they would go in through my mouth. To do this, they would clamp a device on my shoulder. There were two "side effects" that could happen. The first was the possibility that they could break one or more of my teeth. That one was easy to take care of—I have dentures! The second possibility was that my jaw might end up getting broken. Well, I couldn't take my jaw out like I could my teeth, but I told the doctor that I didn't care. I *had* to be able to breathe.

I was becoming a pro at this whole "surgery thing," and I made it through yet another one. When I woke up in the recovery room, I noticed right away that they had fixed the problem. I could breathe freely! The one thing that puzzled me, though, was that I had a big bandage on my throat. I was definitely not prepared for what they had found. Peggy shared with me that while I was in surgery, my original trauma surgeon and the Respiratory Department head came into the waiting room looking for her. They both had tears in their eyes. My trauma doctor told Peggy that they had ruined everything they had done for me.

Of course, Peggy thought the worst, but she asked if I was alive anyway. They assured her that I was fine, and then they explained what they found during the operation. You see, trauma doctors rarely work with tracheotomies; the respiratory specialists are the ones that always deal with them. When my trauma doctor pulled out the tracheotomy plug after my first week at home, she didn't know that there was a second part to it. In addition to the plug, there is a hollow tube that the plug slides into. Come to find out, that tube had fallen down into my esophagus and wedged itself in there. Scar tissue then started growing around it, cutting off my airway and causing my breathing difficulties.

As they were explaining to Peggy what they found, she could tell that they *truly* felt horrible for what I had gone through. Some later said that they were probably just trying to make it look like they cared because they didn't want us to file a lawsuit. We can honestly say that a lawsuit never crossed our minds. We were very impressed with how each member of the hospital staff at the Mayo Clinic truly cared for each patient and their family. From the top doc-tors all the way down to the cleaning people—the whole staff was very impressive. As I've said before, they all had a servant's heart and went well out of their way to make all of us comfortable—during all of our stays there. Peggy told them that we believed the Mayo Clinic was the best place that I could be with the best doctors, especially after the extraordinary things they did to save my life.

After I was taken back to my room from recovery, my trauma surgeon came in and actually crawled right up into my bed and sat down next to me. She explained to me what they found and apologized for what I went through. She told us that we would not receive a bill for this hospital visit.

She said, "But,"—you *have* to hate it when they say "but"—"there is one more thing that we need to check out." She explained that there is actually a third part to the tracheotomy plug—a flat washer that they often slide onto the hollow tube. When they use this washer, it is always recorded on the chart. It wasn't on mine, but she wanted to be *certain* that it wasn't inside me. She took a similar part down to the CAT scan machine to see if it would show up. When it did, she took me to have a CAT scan done. Praise the Lord—there was no washer! Surgeries were becoming second nature to me, but I was more than glad to not have another one just yet.

Not long after that little "breathing problem," I started to notice a lot of pain in my left shoulder. (I wish I was kidding!) We assumed that the morphine had worn off by then, and that was why I hadn't noticed the pain sooner. When we went back for another checkup, I told my surgeon about the pain. She looked at my left shoulder and neck area and decided to send me to a neurosurgeon. So, back to Rochester we went. The neurosurgeon put me through some extremely painful tests. When he was done, he told us he thought that my trapezius muscle was almost completely severed—probably only about 10 percent functional.

We learned that a muscle is like the inside of a golf ball. A golf ball is made up of three parts—a hard white outside, a rubber-band type of material in the middle, and a nickel-sized super ball in the center. Imagine you were to take the outside of a golf ball off, leaving the insides exposed. Then you took a knife and just slightly cut the rubber band wrappings. When you do this, the rubber bands start to pull away from each other. The more you cut, the more it tears and pulls apart. Apparently, muscles work the same way. The neurosurgeon told us the longer we waited, the farther apart the ends would be and the more it would tear, making it much harder to fix. He told us if we were going to do anything about it, we would need to make a decision soon.

We went home that day to pray and talk about it. We ultimately decided to go ahead with the surgery, so we called our doctor to tell him our decision—another surgery. Once again, we made the trip to Rochester. Getting ready for the surgery was *not* fun. They had to stick little electrodes into a lot of the muscles and then shock them to be sure the electrodes were in the right place. Apparently, this would help them to identify the muscles during the operation.

I was in surgery for five hours. Afterward, the surgeon came to us with some bad news. He said that he found all the nerve ends in the neck right away; however, when he went down into the shoulder area, he couldn't find the actual trapezius muscle. It's kind of hard to fix something that isn't there—yes, you heard me right, my trapezius muscle was *completely gone!* The tests showed that the muscle was there, but it wasn't. The neurosurgeon told us that this rarely happens. He felt bad having put me through the pain of surgery for no reason. Because I have no trapezius muscle, using my left arm is difficult. However, I am extremely fortunate to be able to use it at all.

Actually, the neurosurgeon told us that I was very fortunate to even be alive! While he had my neck area open, he saw the damage that had been done by the augers. He told us if the auger had been just a fraction of an inch to the left, it would have severed the nerve that operates the left arm and hand. Most likely, I wouldn't have been able to use that arm ever again; it would have hung limp at my side. Then he told us if it would have been one quarter of an inch to the right, it would have severed the main artery in my neck. I would have bled to death in two minutes. I love telling people that the Lord is the Great Physician. Sometimes He uses different tools to do delicate surgery—He used a sixteen-inch auger to operate on my neck. Once again, it was a sign that God is in complete control of everything in my life. I can trust Him through every situation.

Thanksgiving Came Early this Year

*T*here are three dates that I will always remember. The first is June 9th—the day the accident happened. The second is July 9th—the day I got out of the hospital. The third date is August 9th—my birthday. More significantly though, that was the first day that I looked in the mirror to see the damage that had been done to me. I don't know why it took so long for me to do it, but it just did. This again was another turning point in my healing.

When my dad had heard about our neighbors putting our crops up while I was in the hospital, he was almost as grateful as we were! He bought a pig and planned to have a hog roast when I got out of the hospital to thank the community for what they did for us. The following is an invitation that we put in our local paper, the *Barron News Shield*, on Wednesday, August 5, 1998.

Family, Friends, Neighbors of Dennis & Peggy Robinson

On June 9th, a farm accident changed the lives of our family.

First of all, a special thanks to the first responders and ambulance crew who helped save Dennis' life by arriving so quickly.

To begin with, we didn't know if Dennis was going to live as a result of his injuries.

Peggy and the family spent many days and nights at the hospital in Rochester.

Thanks to all of you, the work at home continued. Farm chores were done, haying was completed, helpers were fed, and Peggy's work at the nursing home apartments continued. Our families took over in our absence, and we are truly grateful to all of them.

The hundreds of cards we received helped to ease mental and physical pain. Your many generous gifts helped to ease our financial burden. Your visits both at the hospital and at home have shown us how much you care.

Most of all we praise and thank the Lord for answering your prayers and giving Dennis the healing he has experienced.

— An Invitation —

As a small token of our thanks and appreciation,

We are hosting a Pig Roast at our farm on Sunday, August 16, Beginning at 12:30 p.m.

Family, friends, neighbors and co-workers—
You are encouraged to attend and celebrate with us.

After reading this article, Dan Lyksett from the *Eau Claire Leader-Telegram* called, wanting to know more. When he heard the whole story, he asked if he could come to the farm and interview us. The following article was published in the *Leader-Telegram* on August 15, 1998.

A Day of Thanksgiving

The Robinsons want to show their gratitude for the miracles and the overwhelming support surrounding a near-fatal farm accident.

PRAIRIE FARM – Come Sunday afternoon at the Dennis and Peggy Robinson farm, your hosts will be serving roast pig and sweet corn.

And the talk will be thanks for miracles and the wonder of good people.

It's a celebration, a chance for Dennis, Peggy and their family to say thank you to all the relatives, friends and neighbors who pitched in "with their prayers and their labors," Peggy says, since a June 9 farm accident nearly cost Dennis his life.

By all accounts Dennis shouldn't be here. Late that June afternoon, a battered Dennis huddled behind the barn, bleeding from deep gashes in his neck, side and arm. Most seriously, he was missing the muscle and flesh from nearly the whole left side of his belly.

Caught first by his sweater sleeve and then drawn headfirst between two of the churning augers of a chopper box, Dennis nearly had been eviscerated.

"He was so ground up; he was just laid open," Peggy said this week at their farm nestled in the hills of southern Barron County.

Amazingly, Dennis was able to back the augers off, free himself and call for help. His son, 17 year-old John, responded to his cries, ran to the barn to call 911 and then summoned Peggy. He also called for his brother, Richard, 18, who was working at a neighbor's farm.

"John did real good," Dennis says.

"I was scared: I just tried to do what you should do," John says.

After packing his wounds with towels, Peggy wrapped the bleeding Dennis in her arms and talked to him and Richard and John as they waited for the ambulance.

"I told the boys, 'We have to pray for Daddy. That's the only thing that's going to help him," Peggy says, "And Denny knew we were there. I told him, 'You can't die. God knows how much we need you.'"

Dennis, now recovering at home after spending a month in the hospital, including two weeks in intensive care, said the accident "tore me all around and chewed me to shreds."

He said one of the ambulance personnel who helped take him to Barron Memorial Medical Center told him later, "I knew you were gone."

Even at that point, however, Dennis was amazing observers with his strength and stamina. Roger Amdall, a neighbor, police officer and firefighter, was one of the first on the scene.

"Dennis was hurt bad," Amdall says, but "he was talking and tried to be in good spirits. It was something like I'd never seen before."

Stabilized in Barron, Dennis was transferred to Eau Claire and then flown to St. Mary's Hospital in Rochester, Minn. After hours of surgery, Peggy said a surgeon approached her and said, "We need to pray for your husband. If anything is going to take his life, it will be infection."

The auger had chewed the left side of Dennis' belly away to the very membrane that contains the organs. Surgeons cleaned and stitched his numerous deep cuts and cut away what was left of the muscle and flesh around his belly, all the while removing handfuls of bacteria-rich haylage from his stomach wound.

"I asked what they did if he got infection," Peggy says. "They said, 'We usually cut it away, but there's not much left to cut away.'"

Not one of Dennis' wounds became infected. The Robinsons call that the second of two miracles surrounding the accident.

The first came during the accident itself. The large main drive chain on the chopper box broke just as Dennis was about to be completely drawn into the machine.

"That's a big chain, a number 50 chain," Dennis says. "There's no reason at all for that chain to break. My body couldn't do that."

"We know the Lord did it," Peggy says.

As awed as Peggy and Dennis are of his personal ordeal and the pace of his recovery, they are just as touched by the helping hands that appeared as if from everywhere when the accident occurred.

"Almost before we got to the hospital (in Rochester) people were showing up at the door here with food." Peggy says.

At the time of the accident the Robinsons still had about 100 acres of first-crop hay to harvest, a critical and time-sensitive resource for a farmer. The neighborhood mobilized. "The farmers got together, talked it over and came up with a plan," Dennis said.

The farmers spent three straight days harvesting hay at the Robinson farm. Peggy said at one point there were loaded wagons stretching from their barn out to the road.

"They said there were 35 to 50 people here at different times, hauling wagons, driving the balers, on the elevators, in the barn—they were all over," Dennis said.

And the help didn't stop there. Recently more people put up another 2500 bales of second-crop hay.

Peggy said there wasn't just work involved but also spirit. She said some farmers who'd had differences for years talked to each other and worked together during the harvest.

And there was sacrifice. The weather cooperated for the three-day harvest at the Robinson farm, but then the rains came and stayed for the next seven days.

"Some of these farmers got our hay up, but they lost theirs," she said. "It shows you what kind of friends we've got."

Peggy and Dennis get as emotional talking about the help of their family and neighbors as they do about his brush with death. Dennis said it's the nature of farm life to help a neighbor, but "it's pretty humbling when it comes back to you."

"It's one of the reasons I like farming and love living in the small community. People pretty much do their own thing, but when it comes to something like this, everybody shows up."

And they say the accident has given them a fresh view of their priorities. Farm safety, for example, is more on their minds than ever.

"For one thing, you don't have to get it all done in one day," Peggy said. "Don't be in such a hurry that you take a chance on getting hurt."

And family, always a priority, has been moved up to an even higher place.

"I think we had a good marriage before, but it's definitely brought me closer to Peggy and definitely closer to the kids," Dennis said. "I re-

ally, really learned that life is too short, and you better take time to, as they say, stop and smell the roses."

So other than the usual mandatory chores, like milking their 23 dairy cows, Sunday at the Robinson farm will be dedicated to the big thank you pig roast. The family, which also includes married daughter Amy Keene, is hoping to have 200 people or more attend what they see as their chance to let people know how much they appreciate all the help.

"I've been able to thank some people that I've run into, but this is a chance to do it for a lot more," Dennis said, "I just want to reach out and put my arms around them all at one time and say thanks for everything they've done."

The day of our party, Sunday, dawned with rain. I couldn't believe it! I was so down I didn't even want to get out of bed. I didn't know what we were going to do with all the people who would be coming, let alone all the food that had been made for the day.

Thankfully, Grandpa Dave's uncle, Bud, had an army tent he said we could use. They brought it over and set it up. Peggy then told me that she had purchased a large tarp a while back, and we could make into a tent as well. I figured "Why not?" They went to work setting that up too.

After going to Sunday school, we came home to help put on the last finishing touches. We weren't sure if anyone would show up, but we had it all ready just in case. Fortunately, we had a very good turnout. It seemed the guests flowed in and out at just the right pace for everyone to be able to sit under the tents. The Lord worked it all out, and it turned out to be a great day.

You know, it's kind of funny that God sometimes uses the most unique circumstances to bring about change. My accident changed not only my life, but it sparked change in the farming community as well. Farming before my accident was all about pride and competition. We were all "self-sufficient." If we *had* to, we'd help another farmer; but for the most part we never did anything together. We knew each other by name, and that was it. In fact, several farmers were on the "outs" with each other. While

I was in the hospital, many farmers came together—several hadn't even spoken in years. That experience totally changed everything. These farmers actually started having block parties and hanging out with each other—what a difference!

"If This is Misery, Bring it On!"

What an amazing feeling it was to thank everyone who helped us at the farm while I was in the hospital. I had come a long way in my recovery, but I still wasn't in any shape to return back to full-time farming. I had to use a walker in order to get around, and I was very weak. I wasn't doing a lot of therapy since there wasn't much there to work on.

Peggy found several folding chairs and placed them around the farm so that I could come out and sit if someone needed to be told how to do or fix something. One day, Peggy was trying to repair the hay cutter. While she was lying underneath it, I was explaining to her, step by step, what to do. It was frustrating not to be doing the work myself because I knew exactly what needed to be done. Even something as simple as explaining which direction to turn a bolt got confusing and made me want to throw the walker away, get down, and do the work myself. I have never been one to just sit back and give instructions.

One day, while listening to the news, I heard about an eight-year-old boy who was killed in a farming accident. They didn't go into any detail about what happened, but I wanted to know more. Thankfully, I was finally to the point to where I could start driving again. I needed to go to town anyway, so I thought I would stop at the gas station and get the local newspaper to see if there was any more information. As I sat in the car, I read the account of what happened.

The boy was helping out at his grandfather's farm. His grandpa had started to unload some corn into the silo and went into the barn to start the milking. Every so often, he would send his grandson out to check on the wagon, and the boy would let his grandpa know how it was going. On one of these checks, the boy went out, but he didn't come back. Naturally, his grandpa went out to see what was going on. I can only imagine how devastated he must have been when he found his poor, little grandson caught in the wagon. The paper didn't say exactly what happened; it just said that his death had something to do with the wagon.

All I could do was sit there and cry. It should have been *me* who died, not that little boy. Why would God let this happen? I learned later that this boy had attended a church's kids program and had recently accepted Christ as his Savior. I know that he is in heaven today because he was a child of God.

❖❖❖

Communicating on the farm was another challenge since I couldn't get around very well. We purchased a pair of two-way radios to help make things easier. For instance, if Peggy had a question while she was up in the silo working, she could ask me over the radio, and I would try to walk her through fixing the problem. Once again, I didn't like it. I knew that *I* should be the one fixing the equipment!

About two months after I came home, Peggy slipped in the barn, hit her shoulder on a post, and tore her rotator cuff. She had to have surgery on her shoulder, followed by lots of therapy. The funny thing about it is that she injured her right shoulder. I hurt my left shoulder during my accident. We told everyone that if you put the two of us together, you *might* be able to find enough good parts for one complete person. Since we both needed rehabilitation on our shoulders, we ended up doing it together. She would do therapy on her right shoulder, and I would do therapy on my left. We made quite the team! Though we didn't realize it then, this was God starting to push us into a different direction.

Over the years, Peggy and I have grown extremely close. I guess we always had a "good" marriage, but we love being together more and more each day. Like we said to my dad, "If this is misery, bring it on!" We both attribute our closeness to our relationship with God. We use a triangle to describe this relationship. The bottom left point is Peggy, and the bottom right point is me. The top center point represents God. The closer Peggy and I draw to God, the closer we get to each other. Unfortunately, the opposite is also true. The farther away we get from God, the farther we draw from each other. This picture shows us our need of a close, personal relationship with God and how it affects our relationships with the people around us.

I spent the next two years recovering from the accident. It's funny that when you're flat on your back, the only way you can look is up. I did a lot of "looking up" in my recovery—both physically and spiritually. Even simple things took on new meanings. I had been driving on the farm since I was 12 years old, and not being able to drive a car made me feel totally worthless. Getting behind the wheel again for the first time was some of the best therapy I ever had. While recovering, my priorities changed. Though I still love to work, it is no longer my god. At the end of my life, I'm not going to look back and say, "I wish I would have worked more." The Lord and my family have definitely become the priority in my life.

These priorities became even more important over the years as our family continued to grow. After Dan and Amy were married, the next addition to our family came when Richard took Rachel to be his bride. They make such a neat couple since Rich is tall and Rachel is short. They blessed us with our first two grandchildren: Alexa and Zachary. We asked them if they were going to give us any more grandkids. They told us that they have gone from A to Z with the names, so that will be it.

We tell everyone that Rich was born with a wrench in his hand. If it has a motor, he can fix it! One time, he purchased a riding lawn mower at a garage sale—the motor came in three boxes. Not long after and with just a little help he had it running. It didn't have a mower deck, but it made for an early version of an ATV. It worked well except when he tried to drive it up a hill on the farm. He ended up flipping it over on top of himself, breaking both bones in his wrist.

Our family grew again when our youngest son, John, married his high school sweetheart, Lisa. They purchased the farm house from Grandpa where Peggy grew up. They gutted the house and rebuilt it beautifully from the inside out. Though it was hard for Peggy at the time to see the home so torn up, it is even more special to Peggy now, knowing that the home stayed in the family and that some of her grandchildren are growing up in the very house she grew up in. We have three grandkids from them: Katilyn, Alisa, and Mark.

John is our outdoors man. He loves hunting and fishing. He has been a great help to me when it comes to anything involving the outdoors. He absolutely loves being in the woods. One day, he came to us and told us he wanted to build a log cabin. He asked if he could take some of the trees from our property to build it. He was only 15 or 16 years old at the time.

I wasn't sure how long he'd stick with the project, and I am pretty stingy when it comes to our trees, knowing that it takes a long time for them to grow back. Well, John started building his cabin; and with help from friends and family, he had it all done by the end of the summer. I assumed his cabin would be just four walls and a roof. Come to find out though, he put a loft in it and even bought a cook stove for it! Thankfully it was put to good use, as he spent many nights up there with his friends and cousins.

Not long after my accident, Dan and Amy moved back to Wisconsin. They, along with their two sons Connor and Logan, are carrying on the farming tradition in our family. Dan was raised on a dairy farm and has always wanted to farm. The main difference was that he did not want to deal with the cattle end of it; his heart was into cash cropping. As a sophomore in high school, he rented his first field, and with help from his dad, he grew his first field of soybeans.

Today they are well-known in their community as one of the leading young farm families. They are currently farming 2,000 acres of their own along with doing custom work for other farmers, consisting of another 2,000 acres. They are also in the process of building a bin site where they will be able to store the grain they harvest.

Amy is Dan's right-hand "man" in the business as well. Along with raising the two boys, taking care of the house, and maintaining a big garden, she has been called upon to drive everything from a tractor to the combine to a semi.

The Lord has blessed us with a wonderful family. Instead of leaving a legacy of hard work, my desire is to leave behind a legacy of what is *truly* important—faith and family.

How Many Second Chances Will You Ask of God?

*T*he Bible talks on several occasions about the "Peace of God." I can honestly say that I have had the most peace in my life since my accident. However, that peace didn't come easily. Since my accident, I have learned many lessons.

First, I learned that life is too short to live with a chip on my shoulder. Hebrews 12:15 tells us, "Looking diligently lest any man fail of the grace of God; lest any root of bitterness springing up trouble you, and thereby many be defiled." If we have a chip on our shoulder or harbor bitterness, it will continue to grow until we deal with it and allow Christ to take care of the problem.

Bitterness is like a tree root. We know that the roots of a tree don't stop when they first get into the ground; they continue to grow and spread out to a very large area. A few years ago, we were preparing to build a church in Iowa. Before we could lay the foundation, we had to clear the land and dig a spot for the foundation. We planned to dig about 16 inches from the original ground level. Unfortunately, there was a tree in the corner of the lot of the church property—and it was a *big* tree. When we started digging, we found that the roots to that tree had spread across the entire lot. It didn't affect just the area where the tree was standing; it affected the entire area around it. We had to get rid of all the roots, or it would have caused our foundation to have problems over time. We ended up having to dig that entire area over 3 feet deep, instead of 16 inches. That's what our bitterness does. It spreads like that tree's roots did. The longer we let our bitterness fester, the further we have to dig to get rid of it later.

The last part of that verse says, "And thereby many be defiled." I saw this happen in my life. The bitterness I held onto affected not only me, but it affected those that were in my life: it affected my relationship with my wife; it affected my relationship with my kids; and it affected those I worked with. I was miserable and I was going to make sure everyone knew it!

One of the biggest changes I have seen is that I don't lose my temper nearly as often—or badly—as I used to. It didn't take much to set me off before. Also, I have more patience with people. I feel that I tolerate more than I did before, and I enjoy spending time with folks more.

Another lesson I learned is that if I am a child of God, yet have unconfessed sin in my life, He cannot bless me. Hebrews 12:6 says, "For whom the Lord loveth He chasteneth, and scourgeth every son whom he receiveth." You know, God has a great sense of humor. I say that because He used a man that I was very bitter toward to explain this verse to me. He shared that the chastening of God happens when He is trying to convict us because of sin in our lives. This sin hinders our fellowship with God because He cannot look on sin.

The gentleman went on to say that the scourging of God occurs when we do not respond to His chastening. He has to go one step further in order to get our attention. When God scourges us, He allows physical circumstances to come into our lives with the sole purpose of getting our attention.

When I heard this, that big, proverbial "light bulb" came on in my head. I realized *that* was what God did to me. I had ignored the chastening. God had to get physical with me to get my attention and force me to get my priorities back in order. To this day, I don't believe that my "accident" was an accident. It was truly the hand of God doing what He needed to get me back to Him. What will it take for God to get your attention?

I guess I have a lot in common with Jonah. God told Jonah to go to Nineveh and tell the people to repent, but he didn't want to. He chose to run away from God instead; so did I. No, I didn't get in a boat and take off in the opposite direction like Jonah, but I put God in a jar on the shelf and ran away from His plan for my life. God scourged Jonah by allowing a literal storm to arise, and He had a whale swallow Jonah whole. God scourged me by allowing a physical storm in my life, and I was swallowed whole by a chopper box. He survived the belly of the whale, and I survived the belly of the chopper box. Jonah finally went to Nineveh, like God told Him to, and Peggy and I finally answered God's calling on our lives. God gave both Jonah and me a second chance (well, maybe more than *one* second chance for me). How many second chances will you ask of God?

I am still by no means perfect. I fail my God every day; but the difference is that I am working consistently to be less bitter, set better priorities, and confess my sins to Him. I also work hard each day to spend time with God and grow closer to Him. This not only helps my relationship with God, but also my relationships with my family, my wife, and the people around me.

I am thankful for what God has done in my life. If my story can help even one person to avoid the pain that I suffered, then it will have all been worth it. I have continuous pain that I live with daily, and the accident left me with many scars. One of them is a daily reminder of

God's place in my life, as well as His sense of humor. On my chest, right over my heart, is a clear and unmistakable "X." I am so thankful I was given the opportunity to be a better dad, grandpa, husband, and child of God. I wake up every morning and thank the Lord for my ... *Second Chances*.

Epilogue

For the next two years after the accident, Peggy and I prayed, asking God what He would have us to do. I knew in my heart that He spared my life for a reason, and I wanted to serve Him in any way that I could.

Once a year, our church, First Baptist Church of Barron, Wisconsin, has a mission's conference where folks come to present their ministries to the church. Some were already serving, and some were preparing to serve in whatever area He has called them. On that Wednesday night, Peggy and I were sitting in the sound booth of our church, listening to the presentation.

As the missionary spoke, God started speaking to our hearts. When we turned to look at each other, neither of us said a word, but we both had tears in our eyes. We knew immediately that *this* was what God spared my life for. He gave us peace, knowing He would go with us through this new phase of our life.

The ministry that was presented that night was Missionary Builders with Continental Baptist Missions out of Rockford, Michigan. This is a group of folks that helps build churches for those congregations who do not have one. We immediately went to work finding out how to join this wonderful ministry.

Our ministry works mainly with missionary church planters from our mission who have gone into an area to start a new church. They usually start meeting in schools or rented buildings. As they grow, they get to the point where they need a church building and can't afford to build one. We also work with other Baptist agencies when there is not a mission church ready to build yet.

That's where we come in. When we come to a place to build, we do not get *any* pay from the church—we are financially supported missionaries. Peggy and I have churches and families who support us financially and also pray for us consistently. From the church's standpoint, we provide our labor for free. This gives the church about a 40 percent savings and allows them to build sooner—instead of having to pay for labor as well, the church only has to pay for materials.

When a mission church has its own building, folks in the area know that it really is a part of the community and will be around for the long haul. It's sad to say, but a lot of people will not go to a church that is meeting in a temporary spot or one that is not nice-looking.

What folks need to know is that the church is not the building that they meet in—it's the people who come together to worship God that make up a church.

Our number one priority is not the building that we are constructing; it's the people who we have the privilege of meeting through the building of the church. Speaking of people, we have been blessed to know so many wonderful people and have made great friends in each place that we have built. We have also seen many come to know the Lord during the building process; and as I've said before, that is the number one priority of our work. Granted, there

are still some things I cannot do because of my prior injuries; but between Peggy and me, we lend a helping hand
anywhere we can.

I never thought that I would be content living in a
trailer, traveling around the United States, and serving
God in this capacity. If someone told me fifteen years
ago that I would be doing this today, I surely would have
laughed at their comment!

It has been so much fun to see the different parts of
our country and meet so many special people. It has also
been unreal how God has provided for us when we have
a need. This was apparent with our very first project. We
were about 60 miles from our final destination when the
transmission went in our truck. I had no idea how we
would get our home the rest of the way there, so I called
our lead builder, and he jumped into his truck and came
and pulled it the rest of the way there. Then, on top of
that, I had no way of paying for a new transmission. Come
to find out, the church gave each of the missionary builders
a gift when they got there. That gift paid for just about all

of the repairs. We have seen God work like that over and over and over.

It has been said that to experience real joy in life, you need to put Jesus first, Others second, and Yourself last. Some of the greatest joy we have had in life has come from serving God with CBM.

It is our prayer that everyone can experience the true joy of serving Christ.